A PHI

A Philosophy of Discomfort

Jacques Pezeu-Massabuau

Translated by Vivian Sky Rehberg

reaktion books

Published by
Reaktion Books Ltd
33 Great Sutton Street
London EC1V 0DX, UK

www.reaktionbooks.co.uk

First published in English 2012

First published in French as *Eloge de l'inconfort*
ISBN 2-86364-631-1
Copyright © 2004, Editions Parenthèses, 72 cours Julien,
13006 Marseille, France

English translation copyright © Reaktion Books Ltd 2012
Translated by Vivian Sky Rehberg
This work has been published with the support of the French Ministry
of Culture – Centre National du Livre
Ouvrage publié avec le concours du Ministère français chargé de la culture
– Centre national du livre

All rights reserved
No part of this publication may be reproduced, stored in a retrieval system,
or transmitted, in any form or by any means, electronic, mechanical,
photocopying, recording or otherwise, without the prior permission of
the publishers.

Printed and bound in Great Britain
by Bell & Bain, Glasgow

British Library Cataloguing in Publication Data
Pezeu-Massabuau, Jacques.
A philosophy of discomfort.
1. Senses and sensation – Philosophy.
2. Human comfort – Philosophy.
I. Title
121.3'5-dc23

ISBN 978 1 86189 903 3

Contents

Preface *7*

one
Discomfort Refuted
15

two
Feeling Discomfort
30

three
Discomfort Dominated
44

four
Discomfort Practised
58

five
Discomfort Denied
73

six
Discomfort Provoked
88

seven
In Praise of Discomfort
103

eight
My Discomfort is My Culture
117

BIBLIOGRAPHY *125*

Preface

It is not the path that is difficult; difficulty is the path.
Simone Weil

Nothing teaches us more about the alchemy of well-being than an old house, particularly one's childhood home. There one discovers the superficial ways in which comfort and its opposite are inextricably associated, like strange bedfellows. In the depths of winter, here I am in mine: an old town house in the Rouergue province of France. Rodents and spiders have established their domain in this icy kingdom, and climbing the four flights of stairs persistently reminds me of my age. Yet I feel good here. My feet easily recall steps and thresholds and each silent room holds a familiar smell. Even the glacial dampness is complicit in the euphoria I call my well-being.

But, one might object, what sort of well-being and what kind of euphoria so easily scorn the home's essential amenities – tidiness, warmth and dryness? From what displaced sensibility do you dispense with them, in the name of some old-fashioned nostalgia? Are you ignoring the progress of hygiene and electronics, as well as the comforts of home technology? I am admonished as someone with old-fashioned tastes and ideas. Words like privation, subjection, nuisance, inconvenience assail me. But I am not worried by these admonishments because I believe such words reflect only the judgement of those who pronounce them; they suggest a negative definition only of a personal and quite different view of domestic contentment from my own.

Few ideas are as difficult to pin down as this. To feel it one must believe it, or so they say. But that's not so easily done. In order to believe in domestic contentment you first have to know what it is, and our existence persistently reminds us of its absence, which is so much easier to grasp – especially since the quest for everyday happiness leaves us forever dissatisfied. Very few perfect moments are left undisrupted by some constraint or other. Once the material, aesthetic or literary components of euphoria are brought together – often at great expense – some annoyance can always arise: a mediocre wine, loud music, a visit from a bore. We are never fully content and the image of contentedness, which serves as our guide, always seems to keep true pleasure at bay. The more we cultivate our *effective well-being* by fulfilling our desires, reducing hardships (or learning to live with them), equipping our interiors, surrounding ourselves with music and books, cultivating our minds and inspiring warm conviviality, the more our ideal image of well-being retreats.

This inexorably remote vision is the image of comfort; discomfort is commonly understood as its absence. But the opposition between the two goes far beyond semantics. First, let's consider their sources. Which of the two terms precedes the other and which should we consider first? In a brilliant study of their origins in eighteenth- and nineteenth-century Britain and the United States, John E. Crowley proposed that the idea of *comfort* appeared with the rise of wealth and as a response to the spectacle of poverty: the perception of their difference was henceforth a sign of social status and respectability. This was the era when Adam Smith famously insisted on the priority of consumption of goods, whether luxurious or merely useful, in all economic life. The cultivated and wealthy classes who alone purchased the former developed a sensitivity to discomfort by combating it through spending, so that those who suffered from it the least became the first to be conscious of it. It is true that each of us (even the poorest) naturally judges our way of living as 'normal' when we consider it in isolation. It is only when comparison becomes possible that desire and fashion urge the rich to acquire things, and the 'less rich', or 'poor', are pushed to resignation or revolt. Revolt is thus founded on the strong feeling of relative ill-being that cannot be diminished through consumption, although it also depends on the no less relative feeling of discomfort when faced with those who are happier than oneself.

Whether or not comfort arises from the feeling of its absence (which I will call 'ill-being'), it is a historical phenomenon and exists only in approximation to a better or worse state that is of the same nature. Comfort cannot be conceived as an absolute because it is simply an awareness of well-being that has ceaselessly varied across eras and civilizations. It has perhaps varied more than its absence has because there are more similarities between paucity and misery (and their finality in illness or death), and discomfort is more uniformly shared than the modes of consumption that allow us to resist it. Comfort and discomfort are not universal, but they have certain properties that transcend time and population, such as the duality of gender and the relationship between the self and appearances and the self and social order.

The impact of the first seems obvious: of all the demands common to humankind, the binary comfort/discomfort remains masculine or feminine in nature. We recognize the traits: men are more attached to appearances, to wealth and to the decor of a building – that is, to what others see – while women remain more concerned with practical and material comforts, a position illustrated by Catherine Beecher (1800–1878), the great theoretician of the modern home. The distinction between comfort and luxury seems useful, if tentative, here: the former, it is sometimes said, is limited to the satisfaction of needs and the latter to that of taste. But aesthetic pleasure still falls under the aegis of well-being, whereas luxury is comparative and is valued more for its rarity than for the wealth it displays. Sumptuary laws have always moderated both through the intention to maintain a certain form of social harmony, about which I will say more. What remains (and is in our nature) is the fact that the contentment we feel remains subordinate to the quest for another contentment that surpasses it. And when we think we might finally take pleasure in this comfort, it is at any given moment threatened by the vagaries of existence – by the actions of another or by our own incompetence. Masculine or feminine, regulated by usages and laws, always fleeting and vulnerable – perfect well-being seems to be nothing more than our preferred Utopia.

Therefore isn't it easier to pursue this pleasure of *inhabiting* (our home, but also the world) on another register, even through the very discomfort that cleaves to our daily well-being? Even if it means submitting to the three ways it affects all of us: privation (due to poverty or restriction), social obligations or outside aggression? And no matter how well we disguise them?

The writer Xavier de Maistre was sentenced in 1792 to 42 days of house arrest and subjected to three states of mental discomfort: solitude, boredom and the privation of freedom. To counteract these he undertook his well-known 'journey around [his] room', which he transcribed in a text that combines humour and melancholy. This journey is primarily a treatment for loneliness, and he writes that one must know how to dream under any circumstances and to trust human nature. Soon his distress cedes to an unexpected happiness, stimulated by the description of the objects surrounding him or the portrait of a deceased friend. Each item in de Maistre's interior opens up a hitherto unknown world of images and reflections where he passes from one discovery to the next. Once his captivity has ended, his final discovery is the understanding that the marvellous struggle of his imagination could only have taken place in isolation and that he can, from that moment on, flee the world of contingencies whenever he pleases. He writes:

> Words cannot describe the satisfaction I feel in my heart when I think of the infinite number of unhappy souls for whom I am providing a sure antidote to boredom and a palliative to their ills. For the pleasure of travelling around one's room is beyond the reach of man's restless jealousy: it depends not on one's material circumstance.

We encounter hundreds of different discomforts throughout our lives and, just like this housebound traveller, we adjust to each of them. Faced with the loss of his free will, La Boétie marks out in his *Discourse on Voluntary Servitude* (1576) the boundaries that nature and God impose on personal sovereignty: revolt turns into a duty against tyranny. When discomfort is of a domestic nature, we decamp, like Socrates fleeing his cantankerous wife. As Nietzsche humorously recounted, 'By making his home life impossible, Xanthippe forced Socrates to speak in the streets and turned him into the greatest philosopher of all time.' Other, less bellicose, reactions to discomfort are perhaps more comprehensible, such as that of the philosopher Gaston Bachelard, who was woken at midnight by the sound of a neighbour hammering. To deal with the disturbance, he imagined he was in the countryside listening to a woodpecker knocking at the trees. And so he returned to sleep, lulled by a 'natural' sound.

We would be wrong to marvel or smile at these reactions. They do not call for a return to the sweet fantasies of childhood, simple positive thinking or reasoned masochism. They do not appeal to resignation or courage or new formulas for happiness at all costs. They merely attempt to grasp and to challenge the true nature of discomfort – at least, the sort we can attempt to cure, and not the distress afflicting much of humanity that is caused by overpopulation, individual or generalized privation, illness, oppression or war, or where extreme scarcity brings about unhappiness or death; only the cynic or the ascetic would find joy in that. In this essay we will deal with the less catastrophic but nevertheless insistent discomforts that disarm and wear us down intellectually, socially, morally or physically.

This quotidian ill-being is as ephemeral as well-being because, it bears repeating, comfort and discomfort are essentially comparative. A house, an opinion, an impression are only *more* or *less* secure than another. Like a self-generating paradox (I am a liar, therefore I am not one, therefore I am one, and so on), the notion of discomfort is dynamic. It declares its eventual duplicity and is only evaluated through successive equivocations. Each of those inevitably leads to a negation, if we know how to distinguish it, and leaves us with a potential exit every time, if we can grasp and extract from these frustrations an eventual satisfaction. This is our natural tendency: we discover ascetic, pedagogical, social or economic compensations in our discomfort, and even a springboard toward new joys. We may deprive ourselves for the benefit of another or deal with people differently.

This essay will try to evoke the different ways we apprehend this discomfort. I am not concerned with boasting the rustic charms of an antiquated thatched cottage, vaunting the so-called values of austerity in the name of some moral or formative quality, questioning the pleasures of luxury, or singing the praises of a monastic existence by pronouncing it superior to the life of the dedicated hedonist. However, if instinct pushes us to avoid discomfort and habit pushes us to deny it, we are still obliged by our existence to recognize it. Could we not use discomfort deliberately or to an advantage that might be pleasurable at a remove? Perhaps we could even desire discomfort (for ourselves or for others on whom we impose it) if we knew how to forge a path through it to well-being. Maybe we could develop a new hedonism out of it. Why not, through the simultaneous management of reason and imagination, integrate these deprivations into our everyday happiness? We could avoid some, transform others into diversions and tolerate those for which the cause seems justified. But first we must reveal the natures of these discomforts and, to that end, must start by naming them.

one
Discomfort Refuted

The Long and Short of It

'Love', psychoanalyst Jacques Lacan once said, 'is wanting to give something one does not have to someone who does not want it.' The present essay, which explores well-being and its absence, takes a similar risk by boldly describing to readers enamoured of their own comfort a reality the author feels he has barely mastered. As with love, we prefer to describe the lack or deficiencies of well-being rather than attempting properly to define it: this everyday amenity of comfort is usually evoked through its opposite. Even so, at least three traps lie in wait for our approach to discomfort. Given its many guises, our most underhand way of pinning down discomfort may be to write about it.

<u>Everything that causes friction or conflict with the material and human environment essentially fits the term 'discomfort'</u>. This can range from an unyielding chair to an abusive over-familiarity and typically includes excessive temperatures, lodgings that are too confined or too big, clashing colours, a provocative painting or book, noisy neighbours, an ill-timed guest, an embarrassing conversation, a lapsing conviction or a feeling of bad conscience. Something as simple as an uncomfortable pair of shoes or a draught of air is all that is needed for us to experience displeasure. Such material

annoyances that directly assail our bodies seem to have troubled our ancestors less. An absence of leisure time and the slow pace of technological progress perhaps heightened the awareness of more pressing needs – housing and nourishment, social mobility and prestige, piety and austerity. Terence Conran dates the notion of everyday comfort to France and to the first overstuffed curvilinear Louis xv armchairs, which were better suited to embracing the forms of the body at rest, whereas across the Channel, the meaning of comfort maintains some of its original meaning and is associated with a more general idea of domestic amenity.

Enjoyment has never depended solely on the self: in every society religion and power have weighed heavily on the personal scales of discomfort and pleasure. Still, where basic sensations are concerned, consider the dual attitude of the Catholic Church with respect to colour: whereas Calvinism prescribed an austere chromatic palette of blacks, greys or deep blues, which still remains the unalterable canon for men's business suits, the Papacy, through its establishment of liturgical colours, then the Council of Trent, and through its adulation of Baroque decor, linked Catholic piety to a profusion of colours that were henceforth legitimized in costume and in the home. In the Far East, Buddhism introduced a severe chromatic palette of beiges and browns into its sanctuaries, but used a riot of golds and reds elsewhere. And all over the world throughout time, political authority has used regulations to establish social harmony, subjecting individuals to housing of pre-determined dimensions, materials and colours which are meant to indicate social rank but also detach us from our notion of well-being.

This essay aims to uncover the nature of the subjections commonly united under the label 'discomfort', as well as the possible virtues or even the secret spark of *jouissance* that lie therein. But added to this vague and growing multiplicity of dissatisfactions is the difficulty of naming them and the appeal of an imprecise vocabulary, starting with the word 'comfort', the meaning of which has continuously changed since it first appeared in French, around 1100 in the poem *The Song of Roland*. In medieval literature, where it is consistently present, the word signifies pity or consolation, but since then its definition has gradually intensified. By the Renaissance, it had already taken on the more concrete sense of an aid or assistance and Huguet's *Dictionary of the Sixteenth Century* (1928) assigns to its verb form – *conforter* (to comfort) – meanings as diverse as to console, encourage, counsel, support, confirm, or to provide strength and to steady. This harks back to its Latin origin (*cum fortis*) and has become common today in French. *Confortable* (comfortable) is an unfamiliar word, but *confortatif* (comforting) denotes the current French ideals of consolation, encouragement and the fortifying quality of treatments and remedies.

It wasn't until the beginning of the nineteenth century that our current understanding of 'home comforts' began to take hold, although the *Littré* dictionary (1885) and the *Larousse Dictionary of the Twentieth Century* (1929) maintained the antiquated meaning. A shift had taken place around 1814, when the English word *comfort*, which had migrated during the Middle Ages, returned to France. While the British conserved its original sense of moral consolation, the Industrial Revolution and the rapid improvement of housing conditions lent it a material and technological edge that it carried back across the Channel. As early as 1815, Chateaubriand evoked 'the comfort of life' with an intimation of physical well-being. The Romantics made abundant use of it, as well as of the word comfortable (as an adjective and a subjunctive). Honoré de Balzac's *The Human Comedy* cites it no less than 46 times, while Romantic author Charles Nodier's *Critical Study of Dictionaries of the French Language* describes it as 'a state of convenience and well-being that approaches pleasure and to which all men naturally aspire'. This is barely different from its current meaning, which always suggests the practical, the intimate and the pleasurable.

Latin distinguishes between comfort and well-being, expressed as *vitae commoditas*, and the comfortable, expressed as *commodus* or *delicatus*, and even though 'comfort' and 'convenience' emerge from different horizons, the latter routinely defines the former. According to the comprehensive dictionary *Treasury of the French Language* (1971–94), comfort is an 'ensemble of material conveniences that procure a feeling of well-being', a definition also adopted by the *Larousse* and *Robert* dictionaries. In 1949 Marcel Aymé analysed intellectual and moral comfort by evoking the 'conveniences that insure the well-being of the mind'. However, around 1650 the term comfort still implied 'utility' or 'advantage'. From the following century, theoreticians and architects assigned to it meanings that increasingly approach ours. The eighteenth-century abbot and architectural theorist Marc-Antoine Laugier understood comfort to include the 'disposition, distribution, salubriousness, and lighting' of buildings. For Etienne-Louis Boullé, 'a pleasant decoration is distinct from convenience', confining the latter to a purely practical function, and Claude-Nicolas Ledoux reproaches French architecture for having compromised 'salubriousness and convenience' through a too radical division of space and the existence of intermediary floors. Today our *comfort* and the *well-being* that results from it (the words and the experience) have absorbed all the material and intellectual 'conveniences' of existence, even if the former has become enriched with highly technological attributes. When qualified as modern, postmodern or domestic, comfort is also a science – 'domotics' – and the engineer, as much as the architect or the decorator, conceives, projects and procures it.

Indecision reigns over the innumerable meanings and the persistently vague semantic quality of the words *comfort* and *discomfort*. The relationship that comfort has established with technology has not clarified things, and there remains an intimate reality that every language has tried to describe. Besides *confort* and *bien-être* (well-being), the French language offers *aises* (creature comforts), *aisance* (affluence), *agrément* (charm), *aménité* (amiability), *commodité* (convenience), *contentement, euphorie, félicité* (bliss), *quiétude, satisfaction* ... and the adjectives *confortable, douillet* (cosy), *efficace* (efficient), *fonctionnel* (functional), *logeable* (habitable), *plaisant* (pleasant) and *pratique* (practical), to name a few. Nevertheless, in using such words we convey only personal feelings that we cannot share with precision. And responses will yield different impressions of well-being or discomfort, dressed in identical terms yet knowing only their own interpretations. As such, we are dealing with the incommunicable and so we must first examine the idea of comfort, its image and impression, before exploring its absence.

The Intimate Dimension – Circles of Desire

According to the American Heritage dictionary published by Houghton Mifflin, the adjective 'comfortable' implies 'the voluntary suppression of all causes of distress or inconvenience'. Mindful of the numerous conditions we assign it, our well-being undoubtedly calls for a less negative definition. Two possible conceptions of such physical and mental contentment come to mind: the first could be called Apollonian, the second Dionysian. The former remains a *state*, a range of comforts and convictions integrated into a position of immobility that we take for stability. The latter is of a more personal nature and involves action: we constantly strive to attain this private form of happiness whose truth consists only in the ongoing certainty that we are moving towards perfection. We may get it wrong sometimes, but isn't it better, as the designer Philippe Starck suggests, 'to commit a creative error than a work of stagnant good taste?'

It is not enough to compensate for the obstacles – whether in form, idea or practice – to comfort. One never attains comfort by satisfying only certain desires (one might also call them instincts or drives) that lurk in the needs whose fulfilment promises well-being. There are four ever-present desires above all: a place for body and mind to exist, a nest and a shell in which they can 'take place'; a decor which reflects one favourably – in one's own eyes and in those of others; a means for the imagination and dreaming to evade the world from time to time; a culture, its ideas and images to affirm the self, even if this is achieved by refuting those ideas and images.

More than anything, we need to accommodate our body in a place. There could never be a theory or use of comfort that does not begin from the body, the group of cells from which we are made and upon which our well-being rests. Everything that motivates or limits comfort stems from the body. Our shelter is built in its image and the space we offer it is nothing more than the amplification of what it already has. Like the body, our lodging will have a right and a left side, a lower and upper level, a front that welcomes and a back that ejects, openings that can close at any given moment. The body occupies the centre of this refuge: only here, while at rest, does it freely experience its physical and kinaesthetic sensations in reaction to the challenges of existence. Each dwelling is a mirror and, as such, reflects only the self.

Of all the qualities a dwelling may have, the most important is its capacity to receive us, to surround us with sides – floor, walls and ceilings – the real solidity of which matters little to our thirst for comfort. We have only to see them to know we are hidden and protected. Certainly, windows open views onto the world and doors allow us access to it. But we can close the former and the latter have no real existence except when in turn we open them (as a springboard to the world) and close them (as absolute protection). These openings define the place of the self, one's interior: they reveal the outside while allowing us to remove ourselves from it. The otherness of the exterior, if not dangerous then at least unknown, forces us to deny it, or at least to distinguish ourselves from it. A shelter allows this. When the self is localized as such, encircled and nestled, it has the capacity for well-being.

But the refuge must first be desirable. No matter how taken we think we are with our solitude or privacy, we only distance ourselves from the 'other' according to our taste or mood. For the sake of personality, and perhaps vanity, we must make a second distinction between ourselves and those from whom we consider ourselves apart. Our home should evoke that. Even if difference is maintained through language or dress, it is taste that remains its dominant signifier and the habitat its primary site for its expression. Whether we opt for luxury with which to dazzle, or austerity with which to shock or displease, it is always a question of distinction, of garnering the attention of others. Examples of this imitation abound and apply equally to a castle as to a shepherd's cottage: all a home needs is to repudiate the frame in which we commonly imagine ourselves (at least in appearance). But are we really designating the 'other' in this way? Form, colour and materials, unexpected objects characterized by luxury or banality, still define the frame of our existence and we cannot escape their influence. By choosing them, by decorating our interior in a particular way, we are perhaps intending to surprise, dazzle or trick the other. But we are primarily modelling our ego and, under the cover of *appearance*, our true *being*. Is this secondary demand for comfort really only a way of displaying ourselves?

It's true that when taken to extremes, decor provides a change of scenery and satisfies another requirement for well-being. Once settled in the expanse of the world and equipped with a specific image of the self, who among us would not occasionally wish to escape, imagine ourselves as different, and elsewhere? Gaston Bachelard considered the home the ideal place for dreaming away the hours, like Aesop's hare. Daydreaming is an activity unrivalled by trips and walks, museums and concerts, and home is where we desire to escape, even from ourselves. This is not difficult: isn't the company of a loved one, a fine wine, an exquisitely played work by Brahms or a jazz tune, a book by Jules Verne or Herman Melville, enough to set us daydreaming? And if one is not wealthy enough to own great paintings or exotic objects from afar, it takes very little – a poster, a photograph, a few flowers – to impart to the home the dimensions of another land. Imagining requires nothing: any space suffices and the emptiest purse is no obstacle.

Still, these evasions must remain brief: such desire does not accommodate itself easily to solitary well-being, tending towards nostalgia and the tenacious reliving of the past. But even this assumes a human presence. The misanthrope or the hermit flees the world only to a distance where they think themselves alone: Alceste's desert (in Molière's *Misanthrope*), Rousseau's island, the poetic solitudes of Alphonse Lamartine, are hardly far from the court or the city; the poet who retreats to mountains or ivory tower still writes for others in a shared language. The need for comfort prevents us from escaping our fellow humans: we have to create our intimate place within our common space. Only then can we make it 'different', or even an object of envy, but this still involves a comparative approach. By creating the refuge of our dreams, somewhere to fool ourselves into forgetting the presence of others, we make progression to this end more difficult.

If every vision of this tranquillity we call our well-being includes customs, conventional figures and received ideas, it is because well-being is rooted in a past where others are always present, and because it is a use or a habit generated by the social body. Memory is structured in such a way as to attach itself to the most serene of past moments. After stamping them with nostalgia, memory reveals them as pleasant features of our daily reveries: recalling a gesture, a recipe or a phrase is enough for us to feel fulfilled and to incorporate it into our lifestyle. Through a particular object, noise or odour, through a garden, book, painting or piece of music, we encounter a reality that belongs neither to the moment of discovery, nor to its innumerable reiterations, nor to the present moment. We only know the timeless character of its essence, as Henri Bergson would say, blended into the self, content to be reacquainted with it. The return of memories indefinably perpetuates a sense of belonging to a group, itself comforting since surrendering to a habit or a custom always fulfils an expectation.

The Many Stages of Comfort

But we are not just dealing with desires in which the need for comfort is rooted. How do we satisfy all the requirements for bliss once we have moved from dream to reality? Once the unavoidable norms of social existence – food, personal hygiene, decency, human interaction or the law – are recognized and observed, well-being is categorized according to stages that can be easily distinguished but whose order we decide upon individually. From a starting point of simple sensation, we encounter the pleasures of the senses, of an aesthetic nature and in relation to others, of solitude or conviviality. Next comes the need for a familiar culture, an environment of images and ideas in which we learn to live.

The Barthesian 'zero grade' of comfort, the comfort of the body, is experienced at the core of purely physical impressions – hot or cold, noise or silence, dampness or dryness, light or dark, agreeable or disagreeable sounds, pleasant or unpleasant odours. Each of these evokes a specific space (of sound, light, or scent) that is occasionally satisfying, but none on its own can recreate the euphoria procured by the simultaneous use of the five senses (sight and hearing impairments accommodate themselves to other forms of well-being). Such contentment appears to be animal in nature. However, if we visualize the Vietnamese stretched out on his hard bunk, the Polynesian in his hammock, the Scandinavian buried in his soft duvet and me in my bed (each feeling perfectly at ease where they sleep), or imagine (absurdly) an exchange of places, we will understand that this so-called elementary well-being depends on more than just our nerve endings.

It depends first on pleasure. The second stage of comfort responds to the demand for beauty, goodness, health and truth that we expect from any domestic situation. The most insignificant object must offer at least something of this: a banal kitchen table has appearance, material and colour whose grain, nuance or sheen can harbour a harmonious or shocking quality; all this is superimposed on its simple utility (which stems from the first stage of comfort). Beauty can even compensate for manifest inconvenience – we sit with pleasure on a hard, Gothic-style chair if we like it well enough or if a loved one has used it. This aesthetic dimension of comfort is shared by each of the senses, from the least subjective – vision (a familiar landscape framed by the window, busy or modest home decoration, the light or dark in a room, colours and textures of objects and walls) and hearing (the quality of silence here and there, the noise of a door, the creaking of stairs) – to the most visceral – touch (of the hand mostly, but also the whole body: the banister, doorknobs, the soft or scratchy coolness of bed sheets) and smell (every house is a bouquet of scents, usually pleasant when familiar, inciting the keenest nostalgia, despite our modern and abusive tendency to cleanliness). The kitchen and dining room hold all the pleasures linked to our sense of taste.

The dual dimension of comfort found in convenience and beauty can only really be appreciated in relation to others, whose participation is necessary in our daily musings. Whether we take pleasure in our distance from them or in their familiar presence, our well-being is defined equally by our choice of solitude or sociability, and most often a satisfying alternation between the two. Solitude has always seduced poets and has become a necessity for health. Torn between one professional obligation and another, jostled on public transport, pressured by the media and the necessity of everyday courtesies, the 'comfort of turning inward' and relying only on ourselves is perhaps nothing more than a simple form of therapy we practise in the isolation of a room or in the warm affection of a familial community. Friends also play a role; the ceremony of the visit is surely one of the most perfect forms of total well-being, combining as it does all the elements we have noted – a sheltered and pleasant physical environment, a visually pleasing practical framework, food and drink and the company of a few loved ones (to the exclusion of all others). Such is the pleasure of conviviality that even when it is dulled by repetition (as with domestic duties, for example), its periodic return perpetuates a belonging that is itself a form of comfort.

Everything that surrounds us demonstrates the totality of a civilization: the decor, the meals, the comments, those anticipated gestures of hospitality whose pleasurable routine we submit to. All of it gently places us in the norms for which our culture has programmed us since the dawn of time. This reassuring environment reveals the final dimension of well-being – invisible but always present, discreet but firm, and which informs our speech and attitudes – intellectual comfort. Except in the company of strangers, we are hardly even conscious of these strict and delicate modes of conduct, which differ from group to group, because education has made them second nature to us. They envelop and guide our conduct to the extent that we hesitate over our true selves: are we the person who speaks (no doubt sincerely) or the one who has learned to keep quiet?

The ultimate stage of comfort should be seen thus: not simply surrounded, but contained, even detained, in a harmonious prison of the conventional terms, shared images and given concepts of an apparent objectivity in which every culture seals its subjects. What we refer to as intellectual comfort has two sides that are contemplated simultaneously: one creates real supports (theories, principles, religions and laws) that assure the stable vivacity of the mind, maintaining a working state between the safeguards that protect it from false ideas and empty words. The other places us under the dominion of unreliable ideologies or seductive words, promising us security of mind and peace in our souls. The former invites critique, then action, and its force is useful. The latter drains us of initiative and creativity, turning moral comfort into a fraudulent imposture of well-being.

The order of these stages of comfort matters little and the fact that some people deliberately cultivate discomfort shows that the balance between them varies. But we must enjoy them simultaneously. True well-being is like a symphony: the individual instruments must not be too loud or too soft; each must be played flawlessly so as not to destroy the harmony. Here I am in my home, in a room that is neither large enough to make me feel 'contained' or small enough to oppress me. The colours in the room are pleasant; it is not too warm or too cold, too noisy or too hushed. I am sitting in my favourite chair, reading a book that interests me while half listening to music that I love. I am not hungry, thirsty or sleepy; I am not cold or hot, nor am I preoccupied with worry or rancour. My body and heart are at peace. Yet if I suddenly felt a draught of air, encountered an unpleasant or poorly written phrase, heard a mediocre trumpeter attempting to emulate Maurice André or Miles Davis, received an unwanted telephone call or found myself visited by a bothersome person, this beautiful ensemble would disintegrate and I would forget all the 'good' elements and fixate on the disturbance instead. Disregarding it would be impossible. It would be like a persistent cloud in the previously clear sky of my bliss. But this is only my own experience: the person who can make the best of the bad soloist, awkward phrase or intruder will be spared and their comfort will remain intact. Furthermore, the association I judged miraculous was perhaps miraculous for me alone. Someone else may take less pleasure in it, or perhaps even feel a certain discomfort.

two

Feeling Discomfort

Discomfort as Privation

The word *privation* is absent from the *Larousse Dictionary of the Twentieth Century* (1931) and it was two or three decades before the standard French dictionary included it. It finally appeared as a synonym for inconvenience and was defined as the simple absence of comfort. However, such a uniformly negative sense only refers to the visible features of a reality or mood that are otherwise complex. The same dictionary defines 'uncomfortable' as 'that which disturbs well-being and mental tranquillity', thus opening the door to a more positive understanding. But comfort remains the sole reference, constituting the only tangible reality as discomfort is reduced to its opposite mirror image. Nothing could be further from the truth. Well-being remains virtual for those deprived of it: its absence is the unique and material truth. Reducing discomfort to the scarcity of comfort and defining it accordingly is to miss its ambiguity. If the most common forms of discomfort assume the characteristics of privation, others are due to constraints of a collective origin, some of which appear as aggressions.

But before it manifests as an idea or an image, an obligation or a form of violence, ill-being is felt in the *absence* of specific amenities, inflicted more or less harshly on the body and mind. All the elements of well-being are present, but only in the background, their deficiency revealing the most negative side of discomfort. The degree of disturbance or unhappiness that comes with this absence has infinite variation and it would be too simplistic to oppose the privations of the young and the elderly (there are undoubtedly ages of discomfort) or the rich and the poor. How we feel them does not depend solely on our wealth or age, our taste or personal culture, but on their association. Between the mortal frustration of the homeless person, who is sometimes so impoverished and dislocated that all sense of regret and of comfort is lost, and the inconsequential privations that accompany a 'normal' everyday life, the rich palette of modes of existence in all societies presents every imaginable nuance of disillusion. The only possible order to make of them seems to be in the categories of well-being.

When we think of discomfort, the distressed or unfulfilled body first comes to mind. The body exposed to extremes of temperature, to thirst and hunger, confined in a makeshift shelter, miserably dressed, unkempt and riddled with afflictions, is a familiar image and, unfortunately, not just a cliché that can be ignored. Troubles resulting from lack (of food, clothing or a roof – in other words, money) are always accompanied by a less tangibly material absence, that of the pleasure of inhabiting or simply living in a place one can call one's own.

The most basic satisfactions – the contemplation or practice of art, the leisure of travel, an uplifting book – are thus refused. With neither the means nor the time to savour these activities, the desire for them can disappear. But beauty and the joy it provides touches all human beings, regardless of age, physical state, civilization, education or taste. The wealthy person who loses a beloved Renoir (by fire, theft or forced sale, for instance) feels as much frustration as the poor person who loses an object of no specific value whose form and colours enchanted them. Moreover, discomfort perverts the messages conveyed by the senses and removes their capacity to procure pleasure. Who wouldn't gloomily contemplate the charm of a landscape from within an inhospitable interior, or one that is too new or devoid of pleasing objects? Deprived of the nostalgia imparted by long-ingrained habits, noises and silence are both powerless to evoke lost impressions. In such a space, poor materials devoid of seduction provide bare necessities and are not agreeable to the touch. And let's not forget the unpleasantness of certain odours, evident when misery reigns in a lodging.

Finally, a cramped, overpopulated lodging does not lend itself to selective sociability. Even if conviviality can soften material hardship, the powerlessness to be alone is problematic. While it does not have the same weight in societies that rely on one-room housing (the Mongolian yurt, the nomad's tent) or where the house permanently envelopes the person (holistic), the inability to be alone is felt most cruelly where a less-pronounced solitude reigns. In the worst cases, a dwelling's overpopulation leads to a dual dysfunction in the family system and the individual soul.

If discomfort deprives us of a spacious and pleasant physical environment, sooner or later it also affects the spirit. It does this in several ways, the most obvious of which is through an alteration of the cultural framework. The feeling of belonging to a people, a society, a civilization (which is evoked by every 'normally' inhabited interior through its appearances, its improvements, everyday lifestyle and our specific rituals) is fragmented and denoted from a distance. Despite the maintenance of a mode of existence based on ties of affection and gestures of subsistence – such as meals – prescribed by a culture, the reassurance of belonging is only maintained through stringent automatism. Corporeal misery makes culture appear commanding, rather than guiding and soothing, and radically reduces the scope of its influence.

Thus the intellectual well-being usually assured by culture is transformed to reflect the three general types of discomfort: privation, obligation and aggression. The first is the most common: the moral framework, which normally provides stability, reassurance and protection, loses its hold on thought processes because the physical environment does not strongly integrate, reassure or stabilize the individual. Our desire for reading, music, entertainment or any other intellectual exchange (which is normally active, critical and always alert) recedes in the face of the simple need to survive. Only the negative side of this moral comfort remains; physical misery, hunger or illness leave us passive and discouraged, neutralize our initiative and creativity and leave us defenceless against the seductions of the word and of soothing and protective ideologies. This is especially true if those ideologies operate in an aggressive or repetitive way.

It is at all levels of sensibility that material discomfort acts as something lacking. But discomfort emerges if even only a single level is afflicted. One false note destroys the harmonious symphony of sensations, conviviality, aesthetic and intellectual joys onto which we project our blissful, domestic ideal, and even more so when there is nobody to sympathize with us. The everyday contentment we must invent in order to survive turns into a caricature of well-being in which we try to see ourselves as having attained happiness. We sometimes succeed because the feeling of comfort always appeals to the imagination, even when other miseries are added to the most tenacious of hardships.

Discomfort as Obligation

While this kind of lack mainly affects the poor, there is another category of subjections that affects everybody. It would be excessive to overly distinguish the discomfort of obligation from that of privation or aggression: restraint and violence sometimes overlap and any kind of ill-being is also a form of privation. But in every society, the individual quest for happiness is confronted with customs, statutes and laws that interfere with personal desires and warp our private image of comfort. The search for personal comfort, and above all for its image, is informed by the social body, no matter what its ethnicity. From holistic East Asian nations to Muslim countries to the apparent liberty of American and European societies, control is first exercised in the practices that submit the individual to the judgement of a group. We can never escape observation by our equal, our neighbour, nor by the authorities over whom we have no control. The gods, whose scrutiny is more remote in industrialized nations, remain vigilant for the majority of mankind, interrupting the rhythm of everyday life with multiple prohibitions. I will limit myself to the example of the home.

Living presupposes a certain mastery of expanse and duration. In every nation, nothing is as strictly regulated as space and time, the rhythms and breaks of which are imposed on every private existence. The respective uses of day and night, hours for work, meals and rest, the precepts of geomancy, the application of specific principles of the ordering of public and private space (such as the practice or rejection of symmetry, the orientation of constructions and the laws that regulate them), are prescriptions that none of us can avoid.

Beyond the constraints imposed on dreams, images and individual projects for fulfilment, others weigh on the frame in which those projects are realized. I do not refer only to materials (only the rich build in stone in a country with an abundance of wood, or have slate roofs where tile roofs are common) that nature, knowledge and use impose on us despite our preferences, but also the palette of colours that each nation judges beneficial or harmful and to which we must also adhere. The omnipresence of a colour in a specific country sometimes results in a progressive acculturation through symbolic enrichment (as with the colour red in Brazil), but more frequently this takes place through official or religious sanction (such as white in Korea or liturgical colours in the West).

Architectural rules above all place limits on personal taste and they do so in a thankless way, becoming fixed in norms, construction techniques and artisanal practices that serve precisely that purpose. Every society develops an urbanism founded on religious or aesthetic principles, or fear of fire, that determines the orientation, height and depth of constructions. I will return to the rules imposed on habitation in the Far East. But every country constrains the way we inhabit spaces, sometimes to the detriment of our desires or the comfort of families. It is worth recalling the tyranny of styles to which we sometimes joyfully submit – especially if they correspond to our taste and finances – because we consider them essential to our own outward appearance.

The use of collective housing in myriad civilizations since time immemorial – long before the Roman *insulae* and our large-scale housing complexes – has undermined the individual ability to manage domestic contentment. Above all, it has imposed the will of one person – the architect – who has become the high priest of our comfort. Demographic acceleration and urbanization have vastly expanded the role of the architect. The writings of Vitruvius, Palladio, Ledoux, Viollet-le-Duc and Le Corbusier, along with our modern builders, brandish a 'concept' of living space and surroundings that envelops the intimate and warm reality of well-being in the cold discomfort of theory.

But the imposition of limits on our quest for a place to live (the architect's common principles, codes and restrictions) also affects our thinking and forestalls our autonomy as we work to adapt. It is only possible to know how to live – to imagine, project, construct and enjoy this well-being – by becoming a social being, one who is historically detached from the institutions, rituals and practices one helped create. They constitute a network of social ties and a common order that weigh inversely on our options. It is only when the individual is integrated in the precise framework of collective existence, in relation to others, that they can fully grasp their personhood and implement what remains of their power of decision.

Habit is the only thing capable of establishing a margin for manoeuvre between my personal choice and social conditioning. Only habit can relieve the distress provoked by the antinomy between my personal choice and everyone else's. When obliged to cover my home in a roof tiles of a specific form and colour, to respect sartorial or nutritional customs, or to adhere to a religious or political practice against my wishes, I will eliminate the moral discomfort of these obligations by turning them into automatic behaviours. I therefore construct a 'free' pseudo-self and preserve a semblance of existential comfort while remaining prone to the game of necessities, norms, divergences and other restrictions of a social origin that have defined me and without which I *would not be*. I will survive inconvenienced, stuck between this false liberty and that half-tamed determinism.

Transforming obligations into habits means they become acquired faculties that allow me to disguise my indecision, navigate between conflicts or contradictions and tailor-make a semblance of freedom. This avoidance mechanism factors into further discomforts of obligation, including those pertaining to place. We know that every inhabited space confers an order on social practices that organize it in turn. But this reciprocity manifests itself in different ways according to the mode of appropriation that predominates. Marc Augé understands *lieux* (places) as spaces where we feel at home, where environment confers its occupants with identity. The *non-lieux* (non-places) are spaces of passage (traffic, supermarkets); they do not identify their users, who therefore remain passers-by. Yet such spaces, open to anyone and rendering everyone anonymous (and temporary), are the constant theatre of consumption and leisure. In other words, their importance becomes comparable to 'true' places like workplaces or residences. But they generate a delocalization that dilutes the feeling of being 'at home' into a derisory multiplicity of non-places in which a contemporary variant of imposed discomfort is visible.

This topological disorder is becoming more pronounced. We live in a time of displacement that is characterized by the settling of nomads, the urbanization of rural populations, migrations related to work, misery or war, dislocation of business and of tourism. Some displacement can be experienced without even leaving the home through the immobile explorations offered by the media. This kind of exoticism (a false change of scene) simultaneously (dis)places us in and outside our homes; we are capable of disappearing because we are everywhere. Augé describes the current identity crisis in industrial societies as a crisis of space: we find ourselves torn from our homes and placed in front of the entire world, thanks in part to the media and cyberspace, which are creating an outsized expanse that lacks signposts and anchoring rituals. The collectively generated discomforts of delocalization and displacement act as impediments that we must bear in order to survive.

Discomfort as Aggression

A third source of ill-being, more severe than simple privation (which mainly afflicts the poor) or social submission (which affects poor and wealthy alike), acts as a physical and moral aggression, whether it strikes directly or in a roundabout way. This is how so-called intellectual comfort operates and, more concretely, it is also how countless dwellings that I have described elsewhere function. I will simply enumerate them here:

First is the *silent house*, even if silent only because of a disagreement. Who has not visited a house or apartment that 'does not speak to them', where they cannot imagine living? The dialogue that characterizes domestic routine proves impossible. This silent space might present all the advantages of veritable comfort: conveniences, modernity, beauty. The door allows us to enter and occupy the space, but the house maintains its unfamiliarity and we don't 'feel' it. In turn, it refuses to receive us.

By attempting to live in such a house we also clash (in a literal and figurative sense) with the *inefficient house*. This house is powerless to shelter us because of its pure and simple inconvenience. Its problems might include location, its relationship to the outside, poor spatial distribution, perilous staircases, corners we get caught upon, slippery floors, absurd storage areas or badly designed openings. Here the architect has spared nothing in discouraging daily existence.

The *half-open house* is neither inconvenient nor dangerous, but simply refuses to become a home because it prevents intimacy. This is due less to the solidity of its walls than to the freedom it denies us. There is no enclosure that would allow its occupant to abandon himself to laziness or daydreaming, free to forget the world. Because of this overexposure and lack of privacy, this type of shelter cannot be a true home.

The lack of authority embodied in the *inert* or *passive house* generates a different sort of mild aggression. The active maternal presence that one expects from a refuge is missing. Incapable of providing its occupant with the feeling they seek by living in it – to dominate it with their own past – this kind of lodging projects misfortune and impermanence. Even when equipped with modern comforts or embellished with objects and fragrances, it remains powerless to respond. We will never be its master or its servant. The union of these two states is necessary for creating a home of one's own.

The *vulnerable* or *precarious house* betrays its occupants by exposing them to discomfort and insecurity. Even if it encloses and contains, dominating us with its authoritative presence, we still require reassurance from it. So we must constantly assess its strength against bad weather and the rest of humanity. In effect, what comfort adds to the facility to forget the world is the ability to let go and fall asleep. The fragile side of a tent can be just as reassuring as the strongest wall, if we trust it. We simply cannot trust the vulnerable house.

The *hostile house* provokes and attacks. When speaking of it, words like *hearth* and *home* are replaced with *mysterious*, *lugubrious*, *sinister* or *haunted*, and it conjures images familiar through a vast literature. Even if such houses do not really exist, if descending ceilings and rigged elevators are uncommon and if phantoms seldom appear, the tales of them suffice to cause disquiet. And let's not forget the real crimes that occur in very ordinary dwellings, where our childhood fears of attacks in the basement or on the dark staircase are manifested within the family home.

The *unhealthy house* welcomes us but only harms us over time. Defective insulation, toxic paints, materials of dubious quality and insidious humidity affect our health and our lives. Of all the unfavourable houses, this is the only one that can actually be lethal. Illness subjects us to one of the most violent aggressions of discomfort, as do depression and all sorts of traumatic experiences that make us prisoners of the past. Here, ill-being is born and perpetuates itself through the regard of others in the guise of emotional insecurity.

Thus we are faced with a discomfort of the spirit that subsists in other forms – and not only in these uninhabitable homes. We can be similarly assaulted when ensconced in the well-being of a normal dwelling, while absorbed in the newspaper or television. A culture dominates through its scientific truths, its administrative authority and seduction by its media, all of which impose themselves on the intelligence of ideas, representations and norms. As I have already mentioned, this often gives rise to mental improvement, the reassuring integration of group values and a barrier against whatever the prevailing culture judges to be harmful or fallacious. But unquestioned authority can also infiltrate us once personal and social control is relaxed. While different to the voluntary deception that I will describe later, the media's constant assault can be regrettably efficient, even if the damage is only felt from the passage of one ideology to another, or when it unsettles our minds and allows intellectual doldrums to take over the home.

Such is the case with the omnipresent discourse on 'modernity' or 'postmodernity': these words are based more in images than in any reality. Rooted in vigorous thinking, this discourse incited a well-known debate between Walter

Benjamin and Theodor Adorno in the 1930s. When taken to extremes it also illustrates the conflict between the appearance of the truth of things and the mirages that power (of any sort) relies on to conceal its own weaknesses. It thus reveals the mild aggression of a type of moral discomfort, which sows the seeds of confusion without offering a palliative. We all know the clichés: the world and society are in constant flux, so unstable, which makes this necessary modernization arduous; techniques and mentalities move at different paces, which is as incontestable as it is inevitable; the permanent revolution (of ways of feeling, speaking or acting) is considered the word-fetish of false intellectual comfort. True logic becomes that of a moving beyond, through which the individual must be divested of the dream and the image in order to invest, which overlooks the fact that every act of projection and construction relies on a wealth of historical representations. The return to flexibility and individuation is imposed – let's turn our backs on rationalism – and this echoes the parallel discourse in architectural neo-modernism. The latter promotes communion with nature via Zen, feng shui or the 'bionic' study of natural construction models in order to capture the vital energy (chi) concealed within them, and denies the pure technologism of the modernist movement that preceded it. These proposals are indiscriminately taken on board in the name of so-called new values or exotic ones whose original foundation and functions are unknown and therefore deprived of their cultural specificity: they harbour an ideological misappropriation.

Even if our new gospels disdain the past and distance themselves from its lessons, their ideas are coherent and active and so, if granted credence, can be conducive to moral comfort. For those who have not lost their capacity to doubt, such claims create a disturbing indecision between the desire to preserve a culture still judged valuable and the seduction of these pacifist revolutions (or other brilliantly packaged chimeras). Here discomfort arises from the act of judging; that is, from putting our norms to the test. Each culture has its own norms based in a system of signs and codes that one must master in order to ward off the aggressions that threaten the spirit. The virulence of such norms can be found in extreme environmentalism.

three
Discomfort Dominated

The Components of Everyday Pleasures

Contrary to the questionable assurances upon which the truest well-being can rest, the frustrations we feel when it vanishes can be beneficial, should we wish to see them that way. This requires education of the will, the imagination and the perception, as well as simple instruction on how to overcome inconveniences. At the most basic level of personal ill-being, this also applies to humiliations that wear us down over time. Here are several examples, in decreasing order of severity.

The sixteenth-century philosopher Michel de Montaigne attributes most of our misfortunes to the imagination, including the then-fashionable theme of male impotence. According to him, this curse was simply the expression of an upset: the soul may be tense and desire ardent, but the body refuses to cooperate. St Augustine thought impotence resulted from original sin, while in the Middle Ages it was blamed on evil spells, but Montaigne's *Essays* (I, 21) denounced the tendency to over-emphasize an image of the amorous embrace so that it became unrealizable in reality. It is necessary to call up other images, first and foremost that of the free will, in order to heal this discomfort. The sexual act becomes possible again once it is no longer felt as an obligation. But for that to be workable, we must occasionally admit our incapacity and feign the renouncement of our virility. Above all we should not promise anything, thus relieving us from the necessity to 'perform' at the required moment, and restoring the soul's faculty of self-determination.

We can remain in turmoil because we fail to practise such exercises of personal liberation. When waiting for a person whose company is always pleasant but whose lateness is irritating, we should not focus on the annoyance caused by the delay, but instead on the joy of waiting and the anticipated pleasure of arrival, which is postponed and therefore heightened. Or we could pass the time thinking about something else, even about our impatience. This hardly alleviates it, but it does open up a greater perspective than simple irritation. It takes very little to reduce a feeling of melancholy when we find ourselves alone: our memories are replete with ideas and images that we rarely think of drawing upon but which would soothe our feelings of solitude, or at least enable us to discover the reasons for them. We might still feel alone, but from a tolerable or even engaging distance. The same can be said of boredom, which Nietzsche asserted 'only active and intelligent animals are capable of', and which immerses us in a persistent and harmful malaise. Regardless of whether it arises from uniformity, as the philosopher claims, this malaise affects us only if we seek the weapons to destroy it from within by taking refuge in the past (as serenely as Russian writer Ivan Goncharov's Oblomov) because of a lack of present or future perspective.

A change of scene is not always pleasant and the discomfort it engenders is often felt most strongly in unfamiliar places. Children, however, know how to transform such discomfort into an adventurous sort of well-being by escaping into the wonder that they can call on anywhere. And why can't we do the same with a book, with Jules Verne or Jorge Luis Borges as our guide? Or, even better, with Lewis Carroll, whose approach seems more conducive to the desired outcome? This brilliant mathematician and logician was persuaded that the mind could not thrive within the confines of those disciplines, so he used their calculations and coordinates to toss Alice into a world that delivers her from reason, scientific topology and language itself. While playing with the clock, with places, traversing mazes and mirrors, she disposes of one form of experience only to be reborn in a liberated space-time that is either free of or filled with landmarks – perhaps in the mode of Walter Benjamin who taught us the art of studious *flânerie* in his book *The Arcades Project*.

If I introduce another person into my personal discomfort, new worries await, beginning with the most ordinary conversation. The verbal expression of my ideas, involving an anguished basic translation of untested thoughts, leads to specific types of intellectual discomfort that are normally mastered through improvisation. Still, how often do we communicate an idea, an expression or an image and yet still feel that there is no appropriate term for it in our own language? And this applies even more so to a new language. How do we interpret an author's (or interlocutor's) conception and description of an idea or object? Each word – ours as well as theirs – couches its initial meaning within a shell of connotations that novelists, essayists and poets have enriched throughout the ages. When *la mer* (the sea) is evoked, a

French person will visualize the painted waves of Courbet or Monet, or they might hear Debussy's harmonies or recall one of Mallarmé's verses, and they will use the word with all these connotations in mind. But for a Chinese or Senegalese person the word will host other images. When 'Dutch interior' is mentioned, I might recall a painting by Vermeer, a strophe of Arthur Rimbaud's *Invitation to the Voyage*, or the memory of a trip to Amsterdam. Based on these choices I will effectively express a different reality to my interlocutor, who will 'hear' something else produced by their own memory.

If I can conquer the discomfort brought about by this mutual lack of comprehension, I can unlock new pleasures, such as the tricky but familiar one of speculating on language. Assuming I know the rules, the satisfaction I might gain by shifting this annoyance into a pleasure seems to be related to my degree of personal culture. An education concerned with individual serenity should provide us with appropriate words and references (a kind of database) in which to anchor indecision, allowing for play. If asked to render *transcendence* or *hermeneutic* into Chinese or Swahili, the most educated person, if they have no knowledge of those languages, will find themselves as helpless as they are ignorant. Their shame will be the greater for their being the only one able to measure the cause. But their knowledge at least permits them this diversion.

Yet more participants can be included in this imaginary game of transforming discomfort into well-being. The discomfort some feel when speaking in public sometimes stems from a lack of vocabulary, as well as the confidence that would permit them to overcome this inaptitude and uncover the pleasure of speaking. Here again, Montaigne's 'curse' and his therapy of distress are relevant: the incapacity is related to speech, but our imagination is still the guilty party, just as with sexual dysfunction. The wait is too long, the desire for eloquence exasperated and the fear of not being good enough too excessive. The wish to seduce or convince a group of people ceases to be tenable if we cling too tightly to it: 'The solicitude of doing well and a certain striving and contending of a mind too far strained and overbent upon its undertaking breaks and hinders itself.' (Montaigne I, 10). As with sex, we must not insist on respecting a convention we have made for ourselves, or on 'doing well' – this only maintains our confusion. The author of the *Essays* admits to having suffered all sorts of feelings of powerlessness, as a man and as mayor of the city of Bordeaux. If he was indeed a responsible and competent administrator it was because he proved himself to be 'sparing with promises' and cautious about taking on more than he could achieve. Perhaps this is a recipe for dealing with our own difficulties. We only really conquer them by remaining open and facing them squarely, before marshalling all our forces to master them. It is not necessary here to be sincere with ourselves: imagination can only be fought with imagination.

A Collective Experience

The discomfort that circumstances, practices or laws impose on us is forcibly integrated into our daily existence; entire societies experience it and master it in their own way. I will use again the example of the home because if our personal subjections are mostly felt in its privacy, the home is also the site of restrictions imposed on an entire nation. The silent house I previously mentioned – the dwelling that 'tells us nothing' and denies us the well-being of living there – can sometimes be found in our own country but it reigns without equal as soon as we approach a different cultural region. Even though a foreign construction might offer a fence, a hall, a bathroom and kitchen, our body refuses to move about it with ease. To attempt to live there would put the entire person to the test; the question of discomfort becomes twofold, concerning the individual and the body politic. The study of *non-places* has shown the extent to which our era offers dramatic or pleasant experiences, but rarely the leisure or the desire to evaluate our mixture of disorientation and fear. Countless narratives of misery or travel deliver vague impressions lacking in objectivity.

From 1933 to 1936, the German architect Bruno Taut lived with his wife in a traditional house in Japan. The story he told about his experiences combines the private feelings of the traveller, the lucid declarations of an honest man and the knowledgeable analysis of the professional. It also provides an exhaustive list of domestic inconveniences – all aspects of discomfort that a dwelling reserves for a foreign user, as well as those for its 'natural' occupants.

Taut experienced these challenges at all the stages of well-being that I outlined earlier. The first challenges were physical: the narrowness of the space in which he lived, a kind of walkway perched on pillars; the need to remove his shoes (the floors were covered with mats); the absence of important furnishings, like cupboards; the constant invasion of bad weather through the gaps left by moveable frames that served as room-dividers or windows. The gestures of living do not adapt well to a space in which the body is a constant nuisance. Taut did not know where to sit, work or seek diversion. Added to this was the betrayal of taste: materials, forms and colours were harmonious but too distant from the aesthetic codes of his own culture to allow him to find well-being in them. He was indifferent to the walls of grey earth, bare boards and joists, and visible structure. Furthermore, the invasion of noises from the outside and between rooms, thanks to the thin room dividers, ruined his tranquillity. Unaware of visiting rituals and the protocols linked to such proximity, Taut could not appreciate the joys of hospitality. None of the signposts that a dwelling uses to guide its natural occupants were available to him: this construction refused to close itself maternally on him. It was nothing more than a provisional shelter, and in no way a 'home'.

With this kind of shelter all of the circles of desire are left in abeyance. The building was fragile, trembling at the feeblest typhoon or earthquake, and did not provide a feeling of security. Taut, knowing nothing of its past, could not invest it with his trust. He had no idea how to feel pride in this home: the criteria of appearances were different and ignorance of national styles meant he could not use them to his advantage. Paradoxically, his desire for evasion was rejected; this change of scene was too radical not to disorient him. Exotic fantasies of his German home, which would normally provide a reassuring illusion, were here reversed in a singularly troubling way. Everything confounded the foreigner: notions of size, orientation, beauty and comfort were established on traditionally different bases and could not be converted into more familiar, universal notions.

That the Japanese inhabitants felt fine there was obvious, and the German wondered at their good-natured acceptance of these difficulties. For them, the tranquil happiness of habit transformed these difficulties into the signs of an observed and revered way of life. This is true of all the world's populations, but these inhabitants did not vindicate the objective discomfort of their homes, which the architect, overlooking his own distress, scrutinized as a professional. Did this type of national dwelling, he wondered, which accommodated perfectly the expectations of its natural occupants, really assure their well-being? Protect their health? Defend them against nature?

At first glance, Taut's assessment seems quite damning, and especially where the construction of the traditional Japanese house is concerned. It has no foundation but is raised off the ground, offering nothing but provisional resistance against storms and earthquakes. Furthermore, the heavy bulk of the roof structure (which requires a piling system specific to the Far East) weighs on the thin wood pillars of its frail frame, adding to its instability. A structure like this, devoid of any oblique element, warps. In winter, the Japanese house is insubstantial, its orientation towards the south rendering it unstable when heavy snow melts on its large roof. Freezing and thawing loosen the stones on which the supports rest; these stones also erode the base of the supports, and termites eat away at the upper reaches.

The interior, closed off with slim, moveable panels, holds its occupants in a no less unfavourable symbiosis with nature.

Humidity and cold reign for several months of the year and the open braziers or hearths in the floors cruelly acknowledge the dwelling's discomfort, especially when compared with the sophisticated heating systems of neighbouring countries such as the hypocausts of China (*k'ang*, often lined with heating walls) and Korea (the *ondol*). But the cold suffered by the inhabitants is to be feared less than the summers. The generous roof of their home is a response to the suffocating tropical climate, yet nothing about it really moderates the heat. The north face, built of masonry, prevents cross-breezes, and thick woven floors block ventilation from lower to upper levels which the pillars on which the structure is raised would otherwise allow. Day and night, intense heat descends from the massive roof in which it accumulates, and the window-like openings above the room dividers or the total removal of these dividers during the day offer no respite.

So an architecture that deprives an entire people of physical well-being has represented for centuries the unique style of housing in Japan. The conversion of its multiple inconveniences (such as the impossibility of being alone) into habits has occurred through their integration into an established lifestyle, irrevocably instituting them across the time and space of the nation. It was only during the twentieth century that the appearance of electrical appliances began to improve things.

Japanese housing is only one example. The Moroccan *casbah* and the Andean *patio* (to which we will return later), as well as our city apartments, offer similar subjections, perpetuated by construction procedures and the integration of practices transmuted into rituals. Their unanimous acceptance upholds a physical lack of well-being that is disclosed in ethnological and medical analyses. Still, everyone appears able to acclimatize and view their particular discomfort as an inevitable, but subordinate, aspect of their way of living. For this tolerance is also a means of conquering the deficiencies that political, social, economic and financial powers have contributed to, if not instituted.

The Mastered Inverse of Discomfort

Thus we can surmount the daily discomfort that circumstances, customs and laws impose. Entire nations such as Japan have learned to reduce it to usages and customs, but in most societies we are not content to be silently enslaved to discomfort. It is possible for political and monetary powers to master it and give it the appearance of a new form of well-being, presenting it to the people as its opposite finally conquered. For a century, we have seen this in the rules and advertisement campaigns that dispense 'conditions' and 'improvements' in our physical and moral health. In addition to the individual control we have our own disillusionment and the common tolerance we show for domestic inconvenience, the public seizure of our discomfort is another way of surmounting it and can be seen as beneficial. At the risk of attacking some of the ideals of our time, I will mention three examples: the paternal dictatorship of medicine, the myth of modern comfort and the cliché of belonging. In these instances, discomfort is considered the negative of well-being and is reassuring because, as we will see, it can easily be alleviated.

Let's consider a familiar example. Nobody is surprised by the extent to which the state, the medical profession or the pharmaceutical industry have interfered with our physical privacy via legal measures, directives or the manipulation of opinion (for example with birth control in China or the question of euthanasia), controls or investigations into our eating habits, personal hygiene or reproductive activity. It matters little that violations imposed in this way stem from discomfort (suffered as an attack against our freedom) or anti-comfort (approved in the name of the common good). Acknowledging the admirable reasons for these measures hardly diminishes their real impact on our physical selves. We do not even perceive the damage because when such measures are levelled at an entire group they evade individual comparison, which is the criterion for all comfort.

Such rulings – and others that can suddenly attribute false moral connotations to moderation in simple acts like eating – have granted those who impose them a quasi-absolute power over our private lives. The justifications for these rules cannot be called into question if one thinks of the prevention of epidemics, the risks of famine due to overpopulation and public health in its entirety. Still, in changing the basic physiological activities of all living beings through such social obligations, these conventions put an end to the propriety of the body and bestow on the doctor the power to dictate our normality – much like the architect, the civil servant, the police officer or the priest. The doctor can thus circumvent our will to choose for ourselves the manner of our everyday well-being or – if we prefer activities that ignore these masters of our existences – its opposite.

The omnipresent myth of modern comfort equally affects us, while constituting a deft stranglehold on its opposite. We witness the triumph of an increasingly necessary technology in domestic life, the growing role of the engineer in the conception of housing, the universal key words of normalization, automation, minimum encumbrance and sensitivity in materials and objects (a clever mixture of minimal materials and surprising know-how). Soon we will see the reduction of services to 'an act of speech and thought', as Philippe Starck says. So many wonderful things are preparing us for an admirable existence.

We generally tolerate the excesses of this postmodernism, which home automation has adopted: overly sophisticated household appliances, superfluous gadgets and imprecisely regulated light, sound or thermal ambiance seem difficult to avoid. It remains that all progress occurs naturally through leaps and ruptures that must be navigated with care. The intrusion of cooking appliances or a television into a traditional setting has always destroyed something, foremost a mode of existence that concerned the entire household and its occupation of the space. The progression from fireplace to stove in Quebec transformed a time-honoured family setting; the arrival of running water in a Laotian village shattered the conviviality established by the trip to the well. Above all what 'happens' in industrial societies, which are prepared for such mutations, will fracture in many others a domestic harmony as ancient as the societies themselves, by imposing a progress that has not yet earned its right to be there. The seductions of convenience and the prestige of machines that come with it cannot be underestimated; some would not hesitate to sell their own children in order to own them. Material discomfort remains the enemy to be vanquished – at any price.

But does the intellectual euphoria (if I can return to this modern comfort of the spirit) that a great number of us ease into arise from this stronghold (exercised by others) on our moral discomfort? Or does it stem from the immediate satisfaction of conquering an untenable situation, thanks to an ideology we claim to follow that protects us from doubt? Psychology shows that uncertainty is a form of discomfort and that we will do everything possible to avoid it – even clinging onto a baseless conviction, or a Utopia. The latter remains more or less necessary, and the flawless well-being of happiness to which we aspire is probably the most widespread. Humanity needs a myth, an idea, a belief, a faith that surmounts, masks or tames all forms of moral confusion, even if it in turn subjects us to another form of constraint – the duty to preserve or defend that faith.

Individualism is the essential dimension of the Westerner; it weighs so heavily on the feeling of well-being that it has become a new source of discomfort. An individual is formed by his or her past, and is necessarily rooted in a so-called continuity. My past thoughts or acts are inscribed in my memory and inform my selfhood here and now. They oblige me to recognize myself in them, so that I respond to a present charged with the past in the public and private dimensions of the individual I believe I represent. In an effort to justify myself as such, I base my own longevity on the age of my culture, affirming that I belong to something outside of which I would not exist, but from which I must nevertheless detach myself in order to be me. Having done so, I substitute an anxious uncertainty with the problem of responsibility, which constitutes the most honourable variation of intellectual discomfort. This pushes me to respond to equally honourable values and to do so unflinchingly because they arise from a culture to which I 'belong'.

Those who persuade us of the importance of these values and our obligation to defend them – the philosopher, the doctor, the professor, the pastor, the political leader – arm us for existence and, regardless of the pertinence of their statements, provide us with a sense of dignity. In fleeing debilitating doubt, we must be prepared to succumb to all possible convictions, such as the discourse on modernity about which I have already noted ambivalence. Because even before convictions are proven well-founded, they give rise to exhilaration; innocent or not, they promise us reassurance and happiness. But first, and as modern bibles of medicine or postmodern comfort have shown, such convictions lead us to believe in the inconsistency of material, intellectual or moral distress. Such distress must be false since we so easily dominate, arrange and tame it into the categories of the good, the well and the true; that is, into a passive and reassuring moral sense of comfort.

four
Discomfort Practised

For the Self: A Profitable Option

It is five o'clock in the morning; I am deep in the warmth of my bed when a strident alarm clock tears me from sleep. A glacial dawn slips through the curtains and nothing obliges me to get up. Still, several minutes later, I am out in the deserted streets for my daily fifteen-minute jog, then I huddle, shaking, in the shower, whose warmth my body does not absorb. Nobody forces me into these acts of discomfort, no form of social control makes me undertake them and I know they have no moral value. However, it never occurs to me to avoid this daily violation of my physical comfort (which is strongly felt and which I can renounce at any moment). I have chosen to carry on, and in doing so, to reject a certain kind of well-being. This is voluntary discomfort or 'anti-comfort'; the inconvenience felt doesn't change its nature or intensity; all that is deployed is the will.

Since I am not a masochist, I expect to be recompensed. My initial pleasure arises from feeling I am the master of my choices, and the more difficult they are, the greater the pleasure. Without forcing myself, I freely embrace three inconveniences that I've already outlined: the *deprivation* of the comfortable torpor of my bed (sleep, heat, warm companionship); the *obligation* to tolerate these attacks (cold, muscular effort); and *aggression*, which I invite, welcome and renew on a daily basis. I supplement these rigours by not refusing them, strongly satisfying my sense of free will. It seems to me to be at its strongest, and my humanity is displayed in these accomplishments since, unlike animals, we want (and do) even the things we do not desire, choosing for example the coldest room, the hardest chair, the dullest companion or the worst food, simply because we are able to make the choice.

But even though my pride refuses to admit it, is this still (above all?) a kind of submission to the dictates of the media or to fashion? In imposing these rigours on myself, am I not also ceding to an omnipresent discourse that it is 'good for the heart' to jog like this every day, that cold water is a good 'shock to my system', and that I am 'hardening' my body and mind and 'sharpening' my will? Similarly, doesn't the gastronomic anti-comfort of denying myself pleasure by eating low-fat cheese or yogurt, replacing the butter on my toast with 'improved' margarine and attentively reading the percentage of fat on every label, articulate another subjection, which also originates in the media, founded on the fear of cholesterol and the danger of lipids for my heart? Or alternatively, attentive to environmental discourse and convinced that humanity is polluting the planet, I might renounce heating and live off so-called organic food ...

However well-intentioned they may be (which we will not evaluate here), the vehemence of these claims I adhere to every day surrounds every space penetrated by eye and ear, as does the eloquence of those who state them and the tide of opinion that they generate. In short, this general assault against my senses contributes to the mental aggression I have described. Part of me knows this perfectly well, but not only do I accept it, I joyfully welcome these modest privations, enthusiastically throwing myself into the facile traps laid by the pseudo-morality of those who espouse them (it is *good* to bathe, *good* to do sports, *healthy* to get up in the morning). I also understand that I am free not to *listen* to the voices that surround me, but how can I not *hear* them?

Still, if an authentic morality really attracts me, couldn't I apply this liberty that I embrace so readily to a more sincere and profound mastery of the self? 'It is not the path that is difficult, difficulty is the path', as Simone Weil says. For I know that one step further in the road to self-sacrifice would provide access to more elaborate forms of solitude and abstinence. There is hardly a civilization that has not invented them as a means of emancipating the spirit. In Japan, doing without food paradoxically strengthens because it represents a victory of the soul over the body. Sometimes such practices are couched in religion. For the earthly benefits of a robust organism we substitute others of a spiritual order that neglect longevity and health. This neglect matters little because the specific goal of anti-comfort techniques is to reduce the material part of the self, whose transitory nature is programmed from the start, to simple survival. Appetites of all sorts are tamed; nothing can stop the progression of thought. A prostrated, kneeling position, which may be painful to begin with, becomes gratifying if associated with spiritual well-being, as does the unquenched thirst that comes from denying the self the sweetness of water (Judaism and Islam are desert religions). These modest physical disciplines take hold in private life; many buildings have spaces for contemplation or sanctuaries containing altars, masks and sacred objects (sometimes passed on from a foreign religion whose powers we incorporate), or a garden we imagine to be Zen.

But even outside all systems of belief, simple solitude invites this mastery of the self. The reverse side of forlorn Romanticism, the 'secret sweetness' of which La Fontaine wrote, well before the effusions of Lamartine or de Musset, is the pure absence of the Other. This is no longer the condition of well-being evoked earlier, rather an anti-comfort, since it voluntarily deprives us of an ingredient of our well-being: chosen sociability. This practice, this 'hermit' state of being alone, not out of misanthropy but in order to better cultivate our own faculties, has been practised by Eastern and Western poets. Without even climbing the Stylites' column, one recalls Robinson Crusoe and, above all, Jean-Jacques Rousseau, who had the character Émile read the exploits of the famous castaway before exiling himself on an island where 'he only has to expend energy on his nascent desires'. Then there is Henry David Thoreau and the French poet Alfred de Vigny in his ivory tower. This type of solitude associates comfort with discomfort in a harmonious muddle in which each soul locates its path alone.

It is no longer a matter of tolerating isolation or embellishing it with the intention to do away with it, or manage it better. On the contrary, we deliberately pit isolation against the sociable part of ourselves in order to practise its obviously negative characteristics: a face-to-face encounter with a disappointing self, the invasion of uncomfortable thoughts, a tenacious moroseness and, above all, the complete absence of others. The ascetic who seeks solitude is never really alone: she has to push aside another who is always present, whom the hidden part of the self desires, and who remains vital to a notion of comfort she has rejected. The game of solitude is not without its dangers and mental despondency awaits the imprudent.

Among its pitfalls is retribution: distancing oneself from the other is still a retreat but the melancholy or anxiety that awaits us turns into contentment once we transform this distance into rest, asylum, shelter or refuge. Or if our needs are for spiritual exaltation, perhaps only reflection can satisfy them, as with the solitude that has long escorted pilgrims along their endless roads. There are certainly constraints, but as with other forms of physical denial, happiness is assured. When these forms are profane, they give the impression of self-discipline; when they are mystical, they provide joys considered to be superior. But however a subjected, accepted or utilized discomfort distances desire and longing, it differs from anti-comfort, which is a practice and discipline. With anti-comfort this distancing only works effectively (especially when communal life is involved) if it becomes a quest for another form of contentment. It is a form of hedonism that must not be taken literally, in which the effort always cedes to the imagination.

For the Other: An Instrument of Submission

This is not always the case. The resolution to eliminate some or all comfort can be applied to others as well as ourselves and can sometimes become imperative or oppressive. As a recipe for authority, penitent or austere anti-comfort can be practised as a group, but our consent cannot always be clearly measured. Whether we are dealing with imposed inconvenience experienced as inevitable (which escapes free will) to that which is inflicted also on the self or only on the Other, there is a personal margin between resistance and submission (between manifested or internal protestation and resigned or enthusiastic acceptance). Both are based in private decisions that reflect social determinisms.

Discomfort shifts to anti-comfort in the name of a precise need, one that is more or less personally felt but, in the case of a group, always collectively approved. The degree of anti-comfort matters less than its nature. We can observe four vindications that reflect restrictions of the well-being of others. These are the vindications of punishment, education (of the child or adolescent), industrial production and group asceticism. Common to all of these are the following: the more or less severe withdrawal of the individual from the life of the world, and their residence in a circumscribed space; depersonalization and the reduction of idiosyncrasies through dress code, a nickname or a number; the shared accomplishment of the day to day rituals of existence; a strict organization of time; the absolute obligation to obey a rule or set of rules and those who enforce them; punishment in the case of fault. These boundaries drawn around our individual peace of body and mind are primarily obstacles to our free will, our immediate freedom to change our options and to make decisions.

Considered from a distance, these rigours all seem alike; we cannot even really determine degrees of severity within them. Whose respective discomforts are more pronounced

– the prisoner or the Trappist monk? This is where the organization of desire (of the subject, the object, the two opposed and mixed together) intervenes and turns decisive. The calculated anti-comfort inflicted on the prisoner, or in a more modest way on the student, the soldier or the worker of the early industrial age, is only a more or less aggressive kind of discomfort for those who can bear it. All it takes is a more humane foreman, warrant officer or disciplinary prefect for the subjection to become tolerable, to turn into a habit or relative form of recognition, placing the subject and object of discomfort in the same camp of anti-comfort. This is the 'Stockholm syndrome' that links prisoners and their guards in fictitious bonds of affection. This type of submission, which is passive or resigned in the case of the prisoner (whose sequestration is imposed), can be observed in students at boarding school or soldiers and workers who are more or less confined to barracks. It only appears complete in the case of monks or nuns, who make their decision with a semblance of liberty.

The discomfort characteristic of the prison environment is supplemented by frustrations linked to the incapacity to leave. The enclosure that defines such a space has expelled freedom: its interior is organized to suppress the image of the outside and the constant physical obstacles there are reminders of its symbolic absence. Compartmentalized, functionalized, its occupant is isolated, naked and imperfectly compensates for this deterritorialization of the body by establishing a new kind of sociability, made up of furtive encounters, friendships and intimacies that are real and often profound, but also ephemeral. Having broken the rules of collective life and therefore threatened the social order, his expulsion from them has been deemed necessary. Lodged and nourished in a Spartan fashion, he is allowed to maintain his physical existence: his punishment and his discomfort are (or should be) only moral. In the case of the monk or the nun, that their isolation is sought rather than imposed does not mean that they suffer in the flesh less than the prisoner. Meagre food, sleep interrupted by prayers, disregard for cold and heat and the obligation to remain silent are added to vows of chastity, poverty and obedience. As unrelenting as the enclosure of the prison environment is, in the monastery it takes on the opposite form. If it effectively encloses its inhabitants in a certain spiritual ideal, it also protects them from a world whose temptations remain ever present, and retains them in the company of others who have chosen the same path and who would not encourage them to renounce it. Physical anti-comfort is commonly pursued in the joy of a constantly shared and sought-after ill-being. This additional custody, in the presence of others, presides over of the acts of existence framed by plain decor and the regulation of time. Of all the great religious founders, only St Bruno turned this collective existence into an asceticism of solitude: in his home, upright and austere, the Carthusian monk faces only himself and divinity.

With most religious orders, prayer and penitence are supplemented by diverse tasks undertaken in the sacred space (work, intellectual research) or 'out in the world'; in this case the door opens at intervals and the rule also takes into account the external function of assistance or apostolate. This can be undertaken in faraway and inhospitable lands. Whether profane or religious, anti-comfort always repudiates that Benedictine 'enemy of the soul', idleness. But the ultimate space for human decision, where individual choice can still be exercised, seems to reside within such voluntary or even imposed rigours.

In its less severe form, anti-comfort imposed on the Other maintains the appearance of simple discipline. From Colbert's rules for the royal manufacture to those of the first industrial age's great factories to the practices of certain Asian firms, we observe a concern with orienting people entirely towards production: their localization (from the family chambers at the Saline de Chaux salt works to current employee housing); their private lives (which was previously 'virtuous and regulated', then simply held in a state of subordination); their motivations and even their souls (in the name of the 'greater good', upheld by the precepts of Confucianism in the Far East). Utopian efforts such as Fourier's Phalanstery or Godin's brilliantly executed Familistère at Guise have revealed the dark reaches of this seizure of individual well-being. The supervision of the barracks or military camp, the secular or religious pension, just like the Cité Radieuse, adopts these givens, generally making it seem superfluous to insist upon them.

The study of anti-comfort, or this voluntary discomfort we inflict upon ourselves or others, demonstrates – by its similarity to the (non-desired) discomfort imposed by poverty, employment or law – the contradictory nature of the displeasing or beneficial object, and of subjection and possible retribution. There are two differences between anti-comfort and discomfort. First, anti-comfort is not just a matter of blindly making good use a posteriori of unavoidably bothersome things or inconveniences. Instead, as we have just seen, those things are a means to self-discipline, education or punishment, or of social conformity and authority. Second, when applied to the self or the Other, anti-comfort operates under the aegis of intellectual and moral assurances (whether founded or not) that cannot be limited without affecting its legitimacy and its efficacy. It is in the name of 'social harmony' and 'justice', or of 'production' (so of 'progress'), the formation of 'responsible' citizens or a higher power (whatever the religion or code of ethics), that such self-denial affirms its *raison d'être*. The only variable is the extent to which the Other recognizes it: from the refusal of the prisoner to the enthusiastic consent of the monk or militant, this anti-comfort can only be exerted through (or on) a group of people if it has first gained the acceptance of every one of them, whether or not they like it. For this reason, a particular anti-comfort must inspire an entire people.

For All: A Recipe for Uniformity

Even so, it is generally from a private place that anti-comfort imposes itself on the body politic. In my previous book, *Demeure Mémoire* (A Home Where Memory Rests), I showed how a domestic dwelling teaches its occupants the ordinary functions of existence. This didactic aspect of our homes (which is always experienced passively) inculcates us with daily rites and family life, norms of taste and, more generally, the values proper to our culture, including its specific notions of space and time. Power systematically captures and instrumentalizes this natural role of the habitation, taking advantage of the confusion over the concepts of family and home and the passivity involved in delegating home design and construction. That being the case, we become indefinitely trapped in the inconveniences that are specific to each type of home. Such subjection – autochthonous or imposed from the outside in the name of tradition or a new, harmful or beneficial idea – always applies *voluntarily* to the *whole* population, with the aim of harmonizing and uniformizing, in order to better control it.

This is true of the Japanese house, my earlier example of a collectively assumed discomfort. But it also illustrates the character of necessity obtained through the imposition of this unique living space on an entire people, whose climates range from the Siberian to the tropics, regardless of natural contrasts. The simplicity of its construction is primarily the expression of a historic poverty that has progressively transformed into an aestheticism of austerity. It is an ideal of sobriety, impermanence and communion with nature that a millennium of poetry and art has relentlessly proclaimed. The contributions of great Chinese architecture elevated the original rustic design in properly national ways (such as the *sukiya* tea pavilion or the *shoin* of Zen sanctuaries). These were assimilated into homes via the relay of the aristocratic residence.

This progressive incorporation of the values of simplicity and rusticity into the domestic space with disregard for material comfort has been constantly controlled and reinforced by human will. Shortages of comfort have been systematized and generalized into an anti-comfort inscribed in the life of the nation and therefore made tolerable. Anti-comfort is no longer felt as such, but is practised as a symbol of national civilization, becoming indispensable to the very act of existence. This is the result of a normalization imposed by the imperial, then feudal, administration which determined the dimension of the mats on the floor at the interior of each fiefdom and regulated the floor plan of each house by submitting the elements of the structure to precise rules of measure. The carpenters were the sole agents of these rules. Moreover, sumptuary laws publicly announced personal status by determining, for example, the length of beams according to function and rank in a strict socio-economic hierarchy. Standardized construction, uniform lifestyle, bodily gestures related to the mats on the floor, became the obligatory basis for all domestic behaviour. Their inconvenience and objective deficiencies were no longer just 'conquered' and reduced to custom, but deliberately harnessed to instil social harmony.

Here we are dealing with an indigenous enterprise. When the discomfort of uniformity is prescribed outside the native territory and introduced wholesale into a different people and culture, it is much less tolerable, particularly since it is frequently imposed in the name of a purportedly elevated or desirable ideal that remains irredeemably foreign. This can occur in an effort to master a society politically, as in the case of China or Japan, or to control it by implanting an unknown religion. A conversion is above all an encounter between civilizations.

There is no dearth of examples. Authoritarian evangelism between the eighteenth and twentieth centuries transformed the civilizations of several Latin American tribes, particularly their practices and sense of well-being, which had hitherto been based in complex and ancient customs. Apart from the imposition of clothing, which destroyed the time-honoured relationship they had established with the body, some were transferred from their traditional huts made from vegetation to unyielding habitations where 'unwelcome promiscuities' could be better avoided. Parked in these shelters, whose materials and floor plans did not correspond to their mode of existence, suffocating under their tin roofs, these tribes lost a lifestyle and domestic rituals that such a space did not correspond to. An essential function of the home – to assemble human beings, behaviours, tastes, affections and belongings – was destroyed. Their new shelters assured them nothing more than material discomforts associated with great disturbances of a moral nature. As late as 1965 (and with disregard for the Brazilian authorities), the agrarian Catholic colony of Sagarana resettled the Wari' far from their native territory on the model of the seventeenth-century Jesuit missions. 'To civilize and to catechize' were synonymous: standard hours and strict clothing were imposed, traditional songs and dances forbidden and punishment was by lock-up. A fire levelled Sagarana in 1970.

Albeit in a less systematic fashion, Spanish conquerors also used housing customs in their quest for political domination. They introduced the Andalusian patio and the mode of familial existence that accompanies it, which is partially founded on mutual surveillance. The Spanish courtyard is visible from the street, probably since the Inquisition. From the tropical heat to the Andean cold, this hollowing out of the habitation standardized symbols, gestures and lifestyles everywhere from Mexico to Argentina.

Ultimately, the use of uniform housing styles takes on the role of maintaining or promoting social order. The geography of the habitat sometimes reveals this standardized semi-comfort of the home. This is evident from the organization of the Western Pentapolis to Mzab (where the Ibadite sect refused any discrimination of a sumptuary nature) to the *rab* erected for the middle classes by the Ottoman sultans; from London terraces to bold housing projects across five continents and the immense sprawl of identical homes in the United States, their density dependent on the average lifestyle of the occupants. We are satisfied to inhabit small or insalubrious lodgings so long as others do the same, the perceptions of (always relative) discomfort dissolving. The good conscience of those who decide is not in question: isn't anyone who exercises a mandate – the state, urban communities, local administrations, employers – expected to house everyone decently and economically? Housed in these almost-comfortable dwellings, our urban populations might be expected to work more efficiently and be less tempted to take to the streets. Once established, such a shared idea of well-being continues to perpetuate itself.

History has shown that this universal seizure of the domestic environment is a timeless imposition of political power, and not only on the house itself. The door in a Chinese home, the height of a chair in Angola, the use of a spoon in Gabon or the secular colours of the Korean interior, even dress code under the Tudors – all communicate a persistent, authoritarian but cheerful, wise but deceptive ordering of material existence, as do norms of temperature, lighting or quiet. And they do so in the name of everyone's comfort – one that faithfully accompanies the hidden discomfort of restriction and law.

five
Discomfort Denied

Oblomov and the Stylite

Whether authentic or misleading, the pleasure of inhabiting (and probably all well-being) seems to be founded on a specific accord between comfort and discomfort in which the latter is often masked, generally repressed and eluding consciousness. Both generate a mode of existence where they operate in conjunction and we cannot separate them. It remains that their respective natures are constantly opposed and we can easily contemplate a lifestyle based solely upon one or the other, with Oblomov and Simeon Stylites the Elder as their emblematic personifications.

Oblomov, the hero of Ivan Goncharov's eponymous novel (1859), chooses to live off revenue from his land. Incapable of tolerating any material strife, or the brutal joys of passion or play, Oblomov discovers a kind of euphoria in total passivity and 'spends his days digging a grave'. Constantly recalling his happy childhood on the family property (on eve of the emancipation of the serfs), he distances himself from anything that would interrupt his tender nostalgia. Although capable of love, he shies away from this assault on his tranquillity. When he finally marries it is only because he submits to the passive delight of being loved. Not fundamentally egotistical, he is capable of pity or tenderness but pushes them aside as soon as they are felt because they disturb his immobile life. His modest fortune accommodates his behaviour, but the deep-seated reason for it is his 'timorous and lazy' character that is 'incapable of enduring the anxieties that come with happiness'.

The fifth-century Simeon Stylites the Elder can be seen as the antithesis to Oblomov. Known for his actions and miracles, Simeon Stylites became the counsellor of the Roman emperors and kings of Persia before tiring of his fame. He decided to live on the top of a pillar he had built and he remained there until he died. From the tenth to the thirteenth centuries he inspired numerous imitators in Syria and Palestine. Like the Indian Fakirs, the Saint Stylites stood or crouched while crowds gathered around the base of their pillars to listen to their homilies or solicit their prayers. This was an asceticism of solitude, which towards the end of antiquity spread in Europe and the Middle East and populated the forests and deserts with hermits. This has nothing in common with the private expectations of La Fontaine, or aspiration for rest or quest for intimacy with nature, even if there is a similar element of desire to distance oneself from the Other, 'far from the world and noise'. A general feeling of malaise reigned at the time, a disorder of a social and moral nature that came about with the disappearance of the great presence that had been Rome. The weakening of a rigorous political framework and the growth of religious freedom led many Christian thinkers to preach the benefits of isolation, of forgetting the outside world, and the practice of meditation.

The enormous distance between the most absolute forms of comfort and discomfort is demonstrated by Oblomov and

Simeon Stylites. The well-fed Russian gentleman, wrapped in his warm housecoat, lying idly on his couch, and the hermit fasting and exposing his barely clothed body to the harshness of the desert, are both fully aware of the state they have chosen. The ascetic seeking physical mortification in order to reach Paradise, and the sybarite surrounding himself with only the most pleasant sensations to acquire instant gratification, have relinquished their availability to others in order to adopt a specific mode of existence. Certainly their paths were chosen from a range of others also determined by their respective cultures. But on finding the one that seemed to them the greatest accomplishment (or to which their resistance was the weakest), they submitted to it without hope of escape, thus abandoning the freedom to change.

Both of them believed themselves to be happy, even if their happiness came at the price of a moral discomfort whose existence they denied but which alone opened the path to that happiness. Oblomov dreaded the loss of his fleeting happiness in a society hostile to solitude. Harassed by his friends, exposed to the traps of love, threatened by the unstable state of his finances, his quietude was never undisturbed. The breaches caused by the inevitable necessity of living in conformity with his time and social class spoiled the serene passivity he had chosen. He undoubtedly suffered more than the Stylite, who at least had nothing to lose, except his health, which Oblomov, conversely, kept under close scrutiny.

One could make a basic interpretation of their uncomfortable well-being. Like numerous mental states, this one is based on a Utopia: regressive for Oblomov, whose happiness depended on the evocation of a joyful past; prospective for Simeon Stylites, whose difficulties prepared him for happiness to come. Nostalgia transforms into hope. The Utopias in which they have sequestered themselves always appear to them as a world of images – relived for the former, fabricated for the latter – but in both cases clung to with idealizing simplification. Oblomov and Simeon Stylites could only experience their comfort/discomfort in the shelter of prisons built of their dreams. Both were similarly satisfied with this sequestering, which as we will see was also a means to observe their lives and to cultivate a particular sensibility (in a Stendhalian claustrophilic way).

Arguably the best-known hermit, Robinson Crusoe demonstrates that a certain vision of the self can allow us to bury deep distress beneath a temporary bliss. Cast without any resources onto a desert island, Robinson Crusoe has to teach himself the bare elements of survival in order to feed, clothe and shelter his threatened body. But this discomfort of destitution awakens in him images of a recent past, out of which he fabricates another well-being, desperately using the images in the same way as the tools he finds on his boat. Inspired by the mercantile ideology of his country and the empiricism of his time (which considered life a series of personal, pious but pragmatic experiences), and animated by a Presbyterian morality and a taming of nature in the name of a God who only protects enterprising people, he transports this recent past into his pitiful present. In his conception, construction and occupation of his cave he mobilizes his persona as an eighteenth-century, bourgeois Londoner.

Thanks to this, his miserable solitude turns into a manner of moral well-being that masks physical discomfort, an ambiguity that many other figures of Western individualism exhibit. Captain Ahab, the monomaniac trapped in his wounded body, reigns like a god over his crew and aims to attain a superhuman state by killing Moby Dick. Instead he ends up a fool, strangled by the rope of his harpoon that the object of his revenge has pulled. Captain Nemo exercises another punishment at sea, pursuing those who have stolen his happiness in his redoubtable submarine. Mourning his family, financing Greek insurgents, intoxicated by music and unblinkingly slaughtering his own kind, Nemo also illustrates the romantic image of a superman even if, unlike Ahab, he dies comforted in the solitude of The Mysterious Island.

In the end, these heroes of the all-powerful exist in a proud, but nonetheless touching, isolation because they are *wounded* heroes. Though endowed with a sort of heroic dignity, and no doubt superficially happy, each is condemned by the constant affirmation of his ego to a fundamental anguish. The unrealizable destiny each has chosen – mastering the elusive beast, taking revenge, dominating or reducing the body to a solitary hedonism, or, like Don Quixote, righting all of the wrongs of the world – imprisons them in images that are nothing more than projections, but onto which their thoughts and activities vainly bestow a guise of objectivity.

Fortunes and Misfortunes of the 'I': The Precious Torment of Self-realization

No matter how enmeshed it is in the values of a social body (even through their rejection), a more ontological vision of the self is concealed within. Rooted in their societies and cultures, Oblomov, Simeon Stylites and even Crusoe, Ahab and Nemo chose or accepted solitude. Like other champions of personal adventure – Don Juan, Don Quixote, Hamlet, Faust, Julien Sorel or Raskolnikov – they accomplished their destiny at a distance from society, more or less by acting against its rituals and taboos. This can be seen as living in a *state of refusal*. Their ordeals, however tempered by their senses of self-worth, were rife with an ambiguity that is even less comfortable and more tenacious because it functions on the level of being as such. Their solitude no longer serves to confront a hostile society, nor acts as a utopian cocoon riddled with traps; nor is it simply egocentric. Rather, the malaise that underlies the exploits of these heroes stems from their decision to live, think and act alone in societies where the simple act of existence remains one of a collective nature. There is certainly pride involved, but above all there is the urgency of the ego that has plagued the West for several centuries.

It is true that today the victory of the self over the group seems absolute and that individualism is the mode of ordinary existence for many nations and peoples. However, individualism was long the object of a sterile conquest, and was always rewarded with multiple humiliations. Opposing oneself to the principles, diktats and practices of the social body (as Oblomov did in the middle of the nineteenth century), or isolating oneself (like Simeon Stylites), presupposed an uncommon strength that turned one into a hero: each manifested the self in an effort that had to be sustained towards and against everything. This brand new 'I', torn from the holism of traditional societies, came armed with singular properties that were either lauded or derided, but was always the fruit of a remarkable effort. It was the 'I' of heroes and saints, delivered by noble cause or turned in on itself like the boyar sybarite in his interior labyrinth. At the price of hostility, he remains egotistically animated by the triple desire to think, act and simply be who he is. Social control, considered an impediment to human dignity and the primary cause of moral discomfort, is thus eliminated.

But today discomfort has shifted. Now it is being alone, free and condemned to individuality that conveys incurable distress. Unlike some African or Asian societies, those of the West are collections of individuals whose fundamental right to remain so is recognized at birth and written into constitutions. Having become a common destiny, this so-called liberation of the person does not reassure our status. It causes fear: we are left alone to confront the fearsome weight of society, incapable of enforcing the rights that belong to everyone.

There is no longer any need to fight for those rights. The energy that was previously involved in asserting oneself in the face of the group, and the forces we assembled to surpass others and ourselves, no longer seem indispensable. We just need to live, to pay our dues, to take what is ours and perhaps to allow ourselves to follow the herd, as Nietzsche said. The alleged comfort derived from passivity and conformity to the common desire to be ourselves is the ransom we pay for a certain kind of individualism. It is felt and practised by the majority, and confuses the happiness of believing ourselves to be alone with the absence of effort.

As the behaviour of our contemporaries demonstrates, this apparent well-being engenders a new form of discomfort whose stages are easily differentiated. The lowest stage is composed of vague but sharp fears of different origins: illness, failure, our friends' troubles, our own insufficiencies and real or imaginary dangers that seem poised to spring up everywhere. The richer the nation, and the less the social body weighs on individuals, the more these fears are felt and the less one seems capable of dealing with them. The endless grumbling of the French, for whom 'everything is going badly' since the origin of their nation (one of the richest and most contented), reveals only a laughable and tragic incapacity to face obstacles head-on and to gain renewed strength from life's ordeals.

This is because it is easy to complain, which additionally procures the suspect comfort of self-pity, something that has become one of life's rules (like the *litost*, a Czech word which Milan Kundera explains is 'the pain that arises from the spectacle of one's own unhappiness'). This perpetual admission of weakness, this humiliation in which we indulge (and which is the second stage of modern discomfort), is visible in our repetitive recourse to those who are stronger or more capable (at least we have been taught to believe that). With respect to the discomfort that arises from doubt, I have described the increasingly important roles of the oracles of our times – the architect, the doctor, lawyer, police officer or priest – whose verdicts leave us a small margin of decision. They have become the sovereign arbiters of our housing, our health, our legality and our beliefs because the fear of living sends us into their arms, turning the people we are into pitiful creatures who can no longer fulfil ourselves outside the shelter of official pity.

Such dependence is hardly reassuring. The third stage of this new discomfort of the 'I' (new in the manner of the *nouveau roman* or *nouvelle cuisine*, but apparently more durable) manifests itself in the fears driven by our dependence, such as our fear of seeing 'legitimate' demands dismissed and of feeling victimized by powers we perceive as intransigent. But we fear even more the spectacle of the dispossession of our cherished individuality by the recurring demands we can paradoxically no longer do without.

Clearly, wanting to be ourselves – or rather deciding that our *being* depends on our individuality – transforms into a positive thing only if we do not watch ourselves live. We are capable of increasing our value as individuals by exposing ourselves to the vagaries of existence and social life, rather than preserving ourselves and fearfully seeking the compensations of turning inward. We must forego this onanism of self-imprisonment and commiseration, which only provides glimpses of well-being – the power to scoff at authority, to have one's rights recognized (perhaps by forgetting the obligations that accompany them), to be pitied by others or, at least, to share common miseries, to collect aid or assistance, to fall asleep every night in the soft bed of our 'advantages', which are just so many new, though unrecognized, subjections.

These illusory satisfactions conceal a discomfort that is generally denied but which several minutes of introspection will reveal as profound and inevitable. It is not a question of comparing the respective merits of individualist and holistic societies, which Louis Dumont has vigorously opposed. People most marked by individualism are also characterized by a profound holism in which they anchor their fundamental values, while others never refute someone's share of responsibility, and therefore existence. But we can see where the cult of the 'I' can lead once it has refused all dependence on the Other: deprived of common rules and reciprocal trust (of mutual *indebtedness*), we find ourselves exposed to all sorts of dangers, real or not, and we are reduced to complaining or demanding. We are less free than we used to be.

The Delusions of Freedom

This existential discomfort or, more precisely, this moral pseudo-comfort of being reduced to individuals (and fallaciously free in our choice only ever to make reference to ourselves) assumes different guises, all of which affirm subservience. This subservience shrouds us in multiple insubstantial and lasting impediments, whose profound and tenacious hold we habitually contest and whose superficial irritation we unknowingly suppress in our deepest selves.

Our new dependence on material things proves this. The consumer age has stripped things of their relative docility and situated our selfhood in their acquisition, not only through their presumed necessity, but also through the glory that technical progress attributes to them and the fantasies that accompany it. Laboratories and factories make apparently flawless products of an irreproachable efficiency; design, materials and colours join forces to exhibit their irresistibility; myths and legends grant them a so-called aura upon which our imagination lingers. They do it so well that banal consumer goods take on the cast of a superego whose domination is continually exercised, while providing the illusion that it is we who are rendered capable of dominating the world. We can no longer hide in the forest of objects; we are condemned to roam from one object to the next in pursuit of some endlessly elusive better thing. This delayed comfort, whose continuous and illusory quest spices up the simple act of existing with petty and incessantly questioned expectations, is primarily a discomfort we feel in the present.

The pursuit of leisure, to which we all seem condemned today, equally expresses this perversion of desire and will. What was first a distraction from work – a more lasting one for the wealthy, sometimes reduced to nothing for the poor, but always desired and considered a legitimate compensation for daily effort – has become a rite, a hedonism of obligation that could even be called a discipline. Our relaxation has been transformed into a consumer good whose use is prescribed and organized by a wide range of new professions, while tireless advertising attached to mirages of delocalization (promoted by television) entreats us to keep on buying. We have become the forced labourers of travel, of cultural or non-cultural tourism, of exoticism at any price, whether our budget permits us to sleep at the Ritz or in a modest caravan. This would not be so bad if, in so doing, we were not submitting our entire behaviour to those who dictate the means of satisfying our need for relaxation, inciting and defining that satisfaction for us. We are left with no real choice, just a false hesitation in the face of their propositions. This perverse variation of discomfort takes on the guise, as do others, of a well-being that pleasingly tinges the subjection or invites us to ignore it. What we are asking of leisure is no longer the exhilaration of a certain kind of freedom, but only to experience the mirage according to a trend and in tones that have been determined without our consultation; in other words, its precise negation.

It is the same with the quest for comfort. Under the diverse conditions outlined in the first chapter, we undoubtedly pursue comfort's real advantages less than we do the illusion of taking pleasure in them and of showing that pleasure. Comfort is reduced to a uniform representation of the home, upheld in the global consciousness of the social body via everyday existence, economic and social life, and the media. We take pleasure in submission because an illusion of personal choice appears to be preserved in it. It would be easy to slide into generalized snobbery, aiming at distinguishing ourselves from others while jumping the queue with the assurance that we are doing things our own way.

However, the radiance with which we adorn our everyday life – including the splendid isolation of our person, the latest, most expensive product, the style and decor of our interiors – is also a straitjacket. Its stranglehold feels gentle or can be ignored because our era makes us think, act and live at a distance from the real, our eyes fixated on signs. Representation and simulation, the avatars of merchandise, have become our sole guides; they are more present and powerful than anything they represent, and have taken the place of reality. Time has lost its density and we live in a present replete with our desires and their more or less fictional satisfaction. We are able to stand squarely in the solitude of the individual consumer and, more accurately, we are capable of *being* entirely real and concrete because of images.

The most insistent of these images communicate our material appearance. The representations that the sybarite and the ascetic create of the enchanted places to which they aspire include those of the corporeal self they will inhabit. In our attempts to deepen our nature as living beings, we first encounter the obstacle of a certain image of the body, chosen among the dozens our era proposes and shares with numerous people like us.

There are many uses for these modes of appropriation of our most physical 'I', and they share a common origin. The 'body as tool' is a kind of capital that must work and remain in shape; its close neighbour, the 'body as machine' must be increasingly productive and needs rigorous education. Then there is the 'body as desirable object', in the name of which we adorn and preserve its relative beauty (by avoiding weight gain and so on), aspiring to a state that will show others how we want to be seen. This is the opposite of the 'feared body' to which the anti-comfort of the Stylite responds: this worrying and rejected body is no longer anything but the dangerous envelope for the soul, therefore it makes no sense to care for it or, worse still, to embellish it. Oblomov's 'euphoric body' is first and foremost an instrument of delicate sensations that one must know how to play, and not without effort or the explorative insistence of someone like Joris-Karl Huysman's character Jean Des Esseintes. It is thus in the name of opposed fantasies that one of them reduces his body to silence, distanced from a world he judges to be bad and in the expectation of future joys, while the other clings to memories of ancient joys that a hostile society no longer provides for him in order to make his body sing.

These images and others with which we adorn ourselves – the image of being independent, a traveller free to traverse the globe, the hedonist occupant of a comfortable home, an ascetic enamoured of austerity – guide us in several ways: they operate as figures of reality (which they reveal in their schematic and harsh way); they bear attributes and symbols that contain their referent, representations of what *must* be; and they impose on our acts a process they perpetuate (as with domestic rituals). Philosophers and moralists use them as a means of persuasion (we know the extent to which Pascal and so many other others relied on metaphor). Finally, they vigorously contribute to diverse types of discomfort, to which we will return later.

Ultimately, these images draw us towards a new and vulnerable freedom, the freedom of the individual we are pretending to be, different from others and draped in the confidence of this regained independence. However, we generally use them in erroneous ways. Concerned with immediate comfort (and forgetful of the determinisms that lead there), we blindly welcome all the guidelines, not considering how they feed off our so-called freedom by inserting themselves into the rut of ideas, tastes and objects that the social body and its culture have dug for centuries. True free will enables us to refuse well-being when it is offered, and to wait for the moment, which comes sooner or later, when we offer ourselves to it without resistance. But we are incorrigible, preferring to deny this subservience because it grants a semblance of happiness that legitimizes for us the imperious seduction of images. Images make us accept the imposture of mirages of happiness. These images are the least offensive; more threatening ones will be examined next.

six
Discomfort Provoked

Images of Discomfort, Discomfort of the Image

There is a further incarnation of ill-being that we must consider. Far from being imposed on us, we seek out its most noxious and aggressive manifestations. It is no longer a question of practising a type of discomfort (for ourselves or others) whose conditions are already present; it is a question of provoking discomfort from a situation where it does not exist in order to gain satisfaction or advantage that would be unattainable without it. No matter the eventual consequences, the essential thing here is to mistreat ourselves.

History and anthropology have shown that premeditated acts of physical or moral suffering exist in every era and every society. The effect of this suffering seems to be a voluntary aggravation of discomfort that is remote to our understanding of it. There are different motivations for it, including spirituality, or a general principle of existence that can entail simple curiosity, environmental protection or the basic will to suffer. Extreme states of this *anti-comfort* sometimes uphold the most severe practices of mystical asceticism. Others, of a seemingly non-violent nature but still as irreducible, simply involve the banishment of material comfort. Still others, which are more damaging, involve the deliberate embrace of everything that threatens our peace and quiet. Certainly dreaming and meditation presuppose some sort of doubt about the individual and the world, and contemplation of the self can suppress a lack and give life meaning. But we can also cultivate this lack and all our imperfections for their own sakes, or simply just in order to see what happens.

Each culture has an art and a literature of excess – one that is mystical or carnal, or deals with passion or violence, eroticism or suffering – and it is always permissible to contemplate this art or read that literature, even if a part of us rejects it. Those who really devote themselves to it include artists, bibliophiles, hedonists, sadists, people with obsessive personalities, connoisseurs of rare sensations and sometimes (why not?) you or me. For most, pleasure is located on the narrow ridge where positive and negative aesthetic impressions intersect, such as in a writer's prose or a painter's choice of colour, and resides in the thrill we feel whenever we dive far off the shores of the true and the good that our sensible societies have marked out with the beacons of their norms.

This voluntary distress, like the unwanted aspects of discomfort, depends on images, but it depends solely on them. Whether they surface from the memory of paintings or from reading (which places fewer limitations on our fantasies), the ambiguous power of images is most effective here. Unlike other types of subjections, where representations drive and justify concrete manifestations (the asceticism of the morning jog or monastic privations, or the imposition of a uniform and unsophisticated habitat on the social body), these images require no material realization. In other words, images cease to be *signs* and become their own *referent*; they use their own power to affect our mental comfort. Who has not felt a certain distress when faced with the accumulation of torturous behaviour inflicted in the Marquis de Sade's *One Hundred and Twenty Days of Sodom*? Or a quasi-physiological malaise at the depiction of a behaviour that our culture has trained us to regard as going against nature (or opposed to its own concept of nature)? We reassure ourselves with the idea that we would never encounter such excesses in our everyday lives, that their outrageousness confines them solely to verbal or pictorial expression. Nevertheless, these thoughts inevitably orient our fantasies towards their eventual realization, indefinitely delayed but compelling in the same way that evil is compelling.

Here we arrive at the source of all discomfort: the power of images to communicate emotion. The fervour with which we accept, provoke and savour discomfort shows that its causes and manifestations rarely stem from outside sources, such as material constraints, cultural imperatives or the will of others. It is no longer an ill-being of exterior origin but one that is born in us, meaning that we can distance ourselves from it only if we do not welcome or deliberately cultivate it. Especially since on the other end of the chain, at the origin of the image, there exists another kind of longing. Isn't its destabilizing power deliberate on the part of the artist? Or does it operate unknowingly and solely through the strength of its narration? Is there provocation or just the sheer pleasure of displaying? 'I have always sought the means to make myself intolerable to my contemporaries', declared Léon Bloy, much as Louis-Ferdinand Céline and so many others have also done. But isn't this affected taste for scandal a kind of powerlessness expressed differently?

This is surely a false problem. A work of literature contents itself with its existence, offering itself to the reader's own imagination, whatever the author's intention. It is hardly the social revelations in Émile Zola's *Les Rougon-Macquart* or the apologetic aims of Blaise Pascal's *Pensées* that seduce us. Reading François Mauriac's novels ('these beautiful venomous flowers', as Kléber Haedens described them), observing the perversions of his bourgeoisie of Bordeaux remains optional. Still, the writer stylizes them in a sombre and harmonious prose that, despite his denials, generates suffocating and frequently depressing imagery.

Art exhibits similar ambiguity. According to Luis Barragán, 'any architecture that does not inspire serenity is an error'. Matisse thought that painting should be like a 'comfortable armchair', and we generally demand that music open up a world of joy and peace. But isn't this misguided? Hasn't the true function of the artist at any given moment been to disturb our everyday life, to provide another meaning to sounds, colours, forms and the 'language of the horde'? Isn't art an essentially heterodox and disturbing means of expression? Returning to the comfort of home night after night is surely a condition of survival, but isn't another demand of well-being the simulated violation of the tranquil happiness of existing? Haven't we all felt the equivocal and scouring pleasure of certain sounds – Stravinsky or techno, it doesn't matter – of colours – Soutine or Soulages – or of surprising architecture? And where fantasy is concerned, what might we say about Georges Bataille's 'divine ecstasy' in 'the erotic autopsy of a live woman' or the painter André Masson's *Massacres*, or even the scenes of torture and rape in Japanese manga?

The thresholds we cross from pleasure to deception, disturbance, repulsion or distress vary according to age, education or mood, and we know that each of these encounters hastens an anticipated clash. The soul's discomfort arrives from three directions: the treatment, style, drawing or colour of a work instantly wounds our *sensibility*, regardless of the talent displayed or the content. But the latter suffices to offend our *moral sense*, as with Sade's novels or engravings of a similar ilk. Finally, the plainly judged work devoid of talent disappoints our *critical spirit*. All told, personal culture and open-mindedness determine the degree of our embarrassment, even when tempered by habit; that is, by our generation. Claude Debussy ravaged our great-grandparents' ears and Baudelaire or Cézanne were equally rejected in their time. This is the case for most true creators, even today. Confusion always incites curiosity, while justifying its attempts to influence nature and to solicit worry over unexpected and perhaps unhealthy things. Still, wished-for and cultivated discomfort only affects our soul and most of us refuse to take it further. One more step would lead us from desire to exaltation, from ill-being to pain, and from the spirit to the flesh.

Asceticism Past and Present

The aforementioned step – from desire to exaltation, from ill-being to pain, and from the spirit to the flesh – is one that leads to absolute anti-comfort. People who attempt to define themselves through such extremes alone never hesitate to take the plunge, while others implement rather less intense forms of ill-being in their defence of diverse ideals. However, it is always a matter of integrating into our physiology the literary or pictorial images with which we are presented, even if they are perhaps no more than exact descriptions. It is true that suffering is most frequently exalted without violence; it even poses as the enemy of violence where altruistic or religious ideas are concerned. The fascination exerted by these representations leads to a redoubtable kind of alienation since it entails the loss of all initiative to return to received sensations, images and ideas. And it subsequently affects speech, gestures and acts.

Take the example of the party. It might seem paradoxical to compare it to asceticism, but both share the capacity to disturb through rites of transgression. The French term *s'éclater* (to burst) and the idea of it (the Dionysian spirit that permits us to lose ourselves) express this chaotic liberation of energies, this occasional desire for auto-violent experiences and a certain drunkenness that always involves temporary but voluntary negation of essential cultural values. More precisely, exalting the Other, which is the dimension of derision, the orgy and of profanation, involves a negation of the visible and 'noble' aspect of culture, as Mikhail Bakhtin brilliantly analysed in reference to Rabelais. The use of some drugs submerges the consciousness and leads to atypical behaviour, causing a generalized liberation of control over the senses that certain types of music can also encourage. This type of collective exaltation is neither ill-being, well-being nor blind provocation, but it leads its followers into an excess of real or pretend pleasure whose role is to offer the (false) comfort of forgetting.

It is precisely the opposite – the fierce will to preserve in memory – that is at stake for those who recommend the new comfort of austerity in the name of the present devastation of our environment. The sole aim of eliminating the causes of ecological cataclysm drives them, even though the current state of science would hardly permit us to turn back the course of industrial progress and history. In its most extreme form, this new evangelism preaches the sacrifice of commodities that rely on polluting energy sources (but which we no longer know how to do without) and the recourse to others, presented as natural (water, sun, wind, sea), to heat, wash and light ourselves or prepare our food. Only management on a planetary scale, whose long process has barely begun, and national politics can master a situation that has become objectively frightening. Every individual approach becomes a Utopia, as attested by the image of the strict environmentalist freezing alone by candlelight in front of their fireplace and sleeping on a thin layer of bedding. This is a candidly futile image, and it would amuse us if only it did not express such profound distress together with such a respectable ideal.

Despite the undeniable gravity of these problems, this ideal is riddled with traps. Multiple diversions stalk the sincere and generous because dual deception is at large. While *ecology* constitutes a science, as Philippe Pelletier reminds us in his book *L'imposture écologiste* (The Ecological Masquerade), *environmentalism* is just an ideology and the *environmental movement* is something else, although both claim the status of the former. But this (voluntary) semantic confusion accompanies another, which it masks and constantly tries to justify. Environmentalism refers more or less to a natural order that encompasses the social or intellectual realms, and which marks a clear fundamentalism. Such conviction – which encourages the undeniably planetary character of the danger and the need for planetary remedies – opens the door to all sorts of doctrines and directions (romantic, conservative, biological, political, sometimes racist or imperialist), all in the name of environmental protection. Such positions frequently present the primacy of nature over culture as dogma and reason (and even the opposite of this in nature or of the historical into the eternal, which Marx stigmatized), or the rejection of anthropocentrism and rationalism (in the name of individuation, decentralization and neo-spiritualism, which also accompanies the neo-modernism I mentioned). These positions can be easily distorted into refusals of progress in general, to pessimism and, since there remains nothing left, to a philosophical or religious sectarianism whose excesses we are familiar with. The physical discomfort and tradition that certain environmentalists predict is minimal when compared with the discomfort caused by these ideologies.

We shouldn't confuse this modern (and possibly dangerous) primitivism with the sincere taste for the antique and worn or unfinished. The Japanese writer Jun'ichirō Tanizaki asserts in his book *In Praise of Shadows* that 'living amongst objects whose lustre has been soiled with grime calms the heart and the nerves'. Earlier, Montaigne wrote of the 'intent, consent and complacency in nourishing oneself with melancholy' (II-20) and considered that 'beggars have their splendour and sensual pleasures, just like the wealthy' (II-13). We are dealing here with an aesthetic of imperfection and denial that is as old as mankind. It is present in every civilization and arises from a classical reversal of norms in favour of a dissident conception of certain values: of beauty (like the 'shabby chic' style of home decoration); but also, when this reverse aestheticism replaces a simple cult of material discomfort, of well-being. In other words, a reasoned practice of anti-comfort.

It is at the intersection of this aestheticism with ugliness that a specific purging function of art intervenes. An example is the potential malaise caused by the fantastic bestiaries made by Romanesque sculptors. The mission of these deformed beings was undoubtedly to make evil spirits tangible for the monks and nuns who were susceptible to profane desires. Symbolized in this way and exhibited in the plain light of the sanctuary, their own interior monsters emerged and disappeared, inoffensive. Dragons, pygmies and the cynocephalus belong to the realm of the night but when manifested in this manner they attest to the existence of divine light. They too are also creatures of God, obedient to him, so that the joy of grace flows from the discomfort of the soul focused on steadily contemplating them in order to eliminate evil.

But these days most of us simply find them aesthetically unpleasant and so satisfy our spiritual needs with more serene practices, although in some cases these may still be abusive. Take certain forms of abstinence, the most common of which is fasting. Almost all religions prescribe some degree of abstaining from food so as to purify the body and soul. Why should we take pleasure in this perishable flesh when more elevated joys await us, especially since this spiritual asceticism often goes hand in hand with the concept of food hygiene? In the name of both these ideas Gandhi described in his autobiography how he kept to a vegetarian diet in England, then in India, reading books that strongly encouraged this. He drank only water, abstaining even from milk. Pushed to extremes, this form of bodily deprivation invites death, but we will return to that point later.

But we can see that the exaltation of going without – food and all other fundamental necessities for existence, including air or light – extends beyond the limits of personal taste, reaching the stricter domain of need and principles. I can fulfil my fantasy of sleeping on a hard surface or practise even more painful physical punishments if I so wish. I can also do it in the name of an aesthetic ideal or a moral obligation that I have adopted. I submit myself to these trials because they originate from someone else's will and are imposed on me, even if it then becomes my own will. Finally, it becomes acceptable to me to practise them on myself or on others for the sole reason that, in my eyes, suffering – my own or that of others – has taken on a positive value.

Exalted Discomfort – At the Edge of the Abyss

In his poem *Vowels* Arthur Rimbaud attributed to the letter 'i' the colour red, the most imperious colour, and richest in connotations (red has more than 500 qualifiers in French). These connotations can be divided into two distinct families where the sources and ingredients of happiness and its contrary can be found. The following, in no particular order, relate to the former: valour, warmth and tenderness, imperial majesty or Christian redemption, compassion, the Red Cross, wine and festivities, the joys of childhood. The malevolent side is equally rich in connotations: blood, carnage, war, impure passions and the flames of hell, fire and financial difficulties. Our choice or rejection of this hue in interior decoration and dress is dependent on our inclination towards either of these series of images.

The Rimbaldian vision stems clearly from the latter: the linear trace of the 'i' (here horizontal) turns into a mouth that draws out female laughter, but from these *beautiful* (and red) *lips* occasionally gushes a spurt of *blood* and the hilarity evoked is that, taunting or cruel, of *anger* (i-re). From the outset, the colour is supported by the plural noun *pourpres* (crimsons), suggesting countless nuances, to which other images in the text attribute the most harmful connotations. This includes the last: *ivresses* (raptures/drunkenness) qualified as *penitent*, that some have interpreted as the joyful repentance of a 'binge' pursued to the point of regret, but this negates the preceding suggestions. One only needs to imagine a torture scene to grasp the extent to which the poet's broken images – the spilt blood, anger, penitence, raptures, uncontrollable agitation or mad laughter – can be coherently integrated into the overarching image of cruelty that unites executioner and victim in a reverence for suffering, the violence of which ends up confounding them, just like in Greek tragedy.

We cannot go on without sketching out the distribution of the pathological and the normal. Both result from a given society's choice to express its common expectations in a specific natural and historical context. A norm (or rule) serves to 'straighten' those objects or facts that are not yet integrated are expected to adhere to it. The norm is only defined in relation to facts or ideas that escape it because they are judged to be of a pathological nature. Normal individuals compare themselves to others who are not normal; normality is only constituted under the threat of abnormality. Since the pathological implies a lack of social adaptation, the normal can only be something positive in a society. The extent to which these definitions escape ethnic or historical comparisons is clear: sexual practices or the particular mutilations that some impose on themselves are judged in our time as bestial and fanatical while in another time and place they may be seen as beneficial. Normal and abnormal are only decided on in reference to a specific time in a specific civilization.

Consider the ideas and practices that surround death. Forgetting that leaving this world is as natural as entering it, some see death as an anomaly born of doubtful medical practices, defective legislation and so on. They mainly see it as the image of absolute evil: the negation of life that follows upon the negation of health demonstrated by illness. There are heroic deaths (on the battlefield), generous ones (in the service of another) and even 'good deaths', but the bleak monosyllable prevails over these heroic adjectives. Some of us avoid it to the point of not being able to say the word itself, demonstrating a fear of language. Using *passed away*, *deceased*, *departed* or *breathed one's last* allows us to swap the unknown joy of the clear and concise word for the futile reassurance of the euphemism. The same goes for circumlocutions like *visually impaired* or *hearing impaired* in place of the more accurate terms for these states of physiological discomfort. We invent the well-being we can ...

But there are others who seek out death, or get very close to it by drawing near to the limit of suffering and thus of life. Of all the body images evoked above, it is the scorned and despised body that uses these techniques of self-sacrifice, amplifying practices already described in relation to self-discomfort. Here, for instance, the withdrawal of food is brought to its extreme. In *A Hunger Artist* (1922), Kafka describes a 'hunger artist' in a circus cage and the disquiet that accompanies any rule of life as soon its traditional justifications fail. In this instance it is a matter of paid discomfort but retribution of another order can be expected when the refusal to eat turns into a ritual of demand. This is customary with children, who reject food to obtain a treat or favour; the prisoner calls it a hunger strike and may carry it out to the moment of death. Its perceived nobility transforms a proud and puerile form of blackmail into an act of heroism. In Japan, the violent and brief discomfort of suicide (I am stretching the meanings of discomfort to their most extreme) is manifested in the moral well-being of reparation. This is achieved either by offering one's life to compensate for a wrongdoing towards society, or by returning precious blood to a homeland that needs to be defended. As Michel Foucault noted, it is a short leap to the dreamlike worship of a superior blood, as with Nazism, and its dual implication of genocide and self-sacrifice.

Christian asceticism, however, which considers fasting to be an imitation of Christ in the desert, as well as a punishment for guilty flesh, strictly refrains from death due to the divine interdiction of suicide. But this apparent indulgence is heavily compensated for with customs such as flagellation. This was first practised in imitation of the Passion, in accordance with the medieval cult of the sacred blood and the quest for the Holy Grail. The Jesuits, with their nascent individualism and sense of personal guilt, made a discipline out of it. While physical effusion no longer exists, we still associate spirituality with the suffering that distinguishes Christianity in the West, and which movements like Opus Dei have taken into this century.

The flagellant 'normally' beats himself, but thirteenth- and fourteenth-century adherents of this practice would beat each other and we cannot separate the pain of the victim from the cruelty of the executioner. If we take the Spanish Inquisition, authorized by Sixtus IV in 1478 and lasting until 1834, we cannot ignore the possible moral comfort felt by the executioner punishing the infidel 'to reason' or the perverse well-being gained from causing another to suffer. In 1591, the Reverend Father Antonio Gallonio recounted in his *Treatise on the Tortures and Torments of the Christian Martyrs* the pagans' cruelty to the first believers in Christ. His list reproduces the arsenal of the Inquisition – wheels and pulleys, presses, hooks, burning shoes – as well as the torments they inflicted: chopping off hands and feet, stretching the body and flaying.

Gallonio attests that the victims' 'greatest desire was to exhale their last breath in the most horrific of torments'. If the burning of Joan of Arc doesn't in itself constitute the guarantee of sainthood, and even if like Nietzsche we doubt 'that a cause for which a man accepts death has something to offer', the de-sublimation of the flesh through self-destructive rituals in countless traditional societies, and more recent examples in which eroticism, mutilation and the quest for abjection go together (as in body art, for example), demonstrates the compelling nature of such extreme acts. And despite (or because of) an abusive feeling of guilt attached to sexuality, the West is never able to free itself from this source of moral discomfort. Here, however, the denial of physical well-being escapes the notion of discomfort; because whether anti-comfort is practised in the name of a mysterious joy of a spiritual or aesthetic order, or for the darker motivation of masochism and torture as sexual retribution, and regardless of whether we judge it as pathological or normal, only death appears to await beyond.

seven

In Praise of Discomfort

The Impostures of Comfort

We can see how these serene or aggressive behaviours resist being given the moral labels of good and evil. Robinson Crusoe manages to create a less material happiness than he ever imagined, as does the Stylite. This is not so for Oblomov, whose punctilious attachment to worldly goods contrasts with their categorical rejection by St Simeon. But hermit and sybarite both experience this pleasurable discomfort by unapologetically distancing themselves from other people. In so doing, their joy bypasses judgements of value, since this contentment and the disadvantages that accompany it are situated outside society and its rules. Isolated in a closed room or at the summit of a column (though each still unknowingly a prisoner of cultural norms), Oblomov and the Stylite escape the verdict of those they have rejected without really disturbing the social order.

And who among us could reasonably judge their respective moralities? To denounce, for example, their servitude to a moral code (in the name of the ideals upon which our value judgements are decreasingly founded, such as Buddhism, Epicureanism, Christianity or Islam) would be to assert a preference for austerity or pleasure, our own submission to another form of determinism. Even if the hedonist and the ascetic avoid such values, we can at least be assured of their equivalent good faith: comfort and discomfort are practised without detour, which is not the case for everyone. Many of us find ourselves abused by the judgement of the group (or by our own judgement) and many practices of sociability provide a mock form of happiness.

Consider all supposedly protective cloistering, the image and idea of which are frequently abused. Initially laid claim to by Jewish communities who preferred to live among themselves and preserve their customs, the ghetto long remained a space of warmth and conviviality, founded on a culture, a set of beliefs and a strong sense of solidarity among the less fortunate. However, even before the Spanish Inquisition, which transformed the refuge into a prison, the true well-being felt and practised there was closed off and depended on exclusion, and even this was primarily based on mutual wishes. The inhabitant's liberty depends on the sole reality that a situation of siege permits or ordains; entirely occupied with desiring what he should want (and forced sometimes to hope for what he doesn't), he is incapable of *freely* wanting what he does not desire, a sign of true autonomy. There is no opposition to the determinism that ties him to his own kind, their choices and their norms. His apparent well-being (which is real on a daily basis) is founded on a secret and profound servitude that leads to an uncertainty of happiness.

We are surrounded by other mockeries of well-being, and even though we contest their insidious malignancy we do not protect ourselves from them. I have already mentioned 'denied comfort' and the misleading tranquillity of intellectual conformity, that immediate certainty that depends only on the approbation of others. Stigmatized by François de la Rochefoucauld, author of the *Maxims* ('It is a great madness to want to be wise all on one's own'), this forms the basis, to a greater or lesser extent, of the function of most of our societies. But we know that it comes at the expense of our liberty to judge, which is the deepest core of well-being. What we call consensus only obtains that quotidian and routine share we need to get through the day. Sometimes the comfort of passive imitation is what motivates the social body, whose judgement becomes the decisive norm for behaviours (for what is good is what is done). The subservience that reduces this ideological dependence lies dormant beneath a conventional, tranquil and cheerful unanimity. Sometimes it violently rebels, but without the strength of the ghetto to open up onto a new form of happiness. But who would judge that necessary?

Under a more material – but no less serious – guise, this false face of comfort entices us with machines that convince us we can breach time and space. It was long thought that the Internet would achieve the utopia of global communication. Instead, it has become a battlefield for the interests of power and money, and led to the fragmentation of human thought, while leaving aside those who cannot access it, or who communicate differently. Cyberspace will make sense only in its universality – when each person has attained in their own culture a level that permits them truly to communicate with all others. We once believed that electronically automating commercial transactions would free them from all legal, physical and customs barriers, as well as moral ones, and that prices would balance out across the network, like communicating vessels. Of course nothing of the sort has transpired and new rules of the market have normalized exchange. This has simultaneously sanctioned the failure of technological determinism and an imposture of comfort, which purports to be founded on material progress.

Discomfort itself is sometimes fallacious. Even the sincere anxiety that comes from poverty, or exclusion from the consensus, the intellectual conformism just described or, more egotistically, the act of contemplating how others tolerate such miseries, has given rise to declarations of principle and inspired poems. In the West we are familiar with countless nineteenth-century tales of misery, the sombre-toned paintings of the life of the poor, elaborated by the glum observation and active hand of well-fed artists with feeling for the 'nobility of destitution' or the 'modest happiness' of the most wretched. This despite La Rochefoucauld's acerbic verdict that 'we all have enough strength to support the evils that befall others'. This constant pity and the tears some enjoy spilling over the miseries of the world (and which also sometimes accompany the false moral comfort of charity) are a feast for the connoisseur of warm feelings and reassuring solidarities.

Anti-comfort itself, the desired discomfort, sometimes takes advantage. The rules and justifications linked to practices of privation, which most civilizations have allotted a place in moral life, lend themselves to a feigned sincerity as much as material comfort does. One thinks of those who live beyond their means and veil the truth behind a dazzling appearance. Yet the ascetic is not always reluctant to show his misery and valour, even if he does not necessarily display them on top of a column. For, if we believe Nietzsche, only the body dispenses authenticity and faultlessly generates a style of existence worthy of man. We have a tendency to haunt the 'swamp of material happiness', alienating ourselves from the liberty of 'indifference from woes and privations'. The modernity we are so proud of is nothing but the sacralization of purely physical happiness. But abstinence is no less compromising: such 'asceticism of morals' only fabricates a pitiful fakery of the 'supple discipline of instinct'. Through bodily mortifications, the penitent triumphs, but this glory only serves to distinguish him from the crowd. He imposes on himself what the 'barbarian' imposes on others, and for the same reason: to emphasize his value.

This is an extreme verdict, and one that might be contested. Still, it lays bare the shams of well-being, its denial and the complacency we bring to it, as with the bodily rejection exhibited by some (the extreme of anorexia representing the pathological form) or the even more toxic seductions of intellectual comfort. All our acts of well-being oppose necessity and sincerity, perilous notions whose rational approach seems destined to failure unless well-being shows itself to be intersubjective and communicative. So in our appreciation of discomfort, it is time to show how it can sometimes be the smokescreen to happiness, a path towards it. It is time, finally, to praise discomfort.

The Essential Mask of Happiness

The potential value of discomfort does not reside only in the negation of an often fallacious comfort. It stems, in a positive way, from inconveniences or everyday annoyances and from the doors they open to a veritable well-being. Much of the euphoria of inhabiting the home and the world would remain out of reach were it not for the specific discomfort that accompanies it, lighting the way.

We know that domestic contentment unites us with ourselves, gathering our diverse belongings into the solid beam of light given off by ourselves and our dwelling. But modern life endlessly disrupts this ensemble. First it deprives us of this true place, either through housing crises or nomadic lifestyles imposed in our time by leisure, professional life, miseries or war. Even when we are sedentary the brutal invasions of modern comfort, the daily immersion in the vague stretch of cyberspace or increasingly rapid transportation and the omnipresence of the media cause displacements everywhere. They do not really help us to live; they physically and mentally disable us. In this situation, true well-being – which corrects and tries to compensate for such disturbance – is only conceived through a more or less palpable distress. Only the skilful management of this discomfort can conquer it: opposing it by refusing to modernize too quickly, to move too frequently, even on the Internet; tolerating it by deliberately placing the self in several places; cultivating it by practising this erring and dissociation for the benefit of other joys.

We put our liberty into play because intellectual discomfort impedes our facility to calmly make decisions, at least about the things that the multiple determinants of existence leave for us to decide. It matters little that this liberty involves submitting ourselves to the canons of our culture in order to put into practice our desire for well-being or, in contrast, that it serves to deny the values of the group in order to choose our own individual hedonism. Here again, wherever our desire takes us, we must first confront, traverse and assume the anxiety of possible alienation: that of becoming the thing we have chosen, of relinquishing the freedom to change, even though the responsibility for our decisions that this freedom gave us was a source of anxiety. Oblomov and the Stylite surmount this double-edged moral discomfort by refusing to belong to the social body or adopt the comfortable usages of social life. But they still have to resist the society they deserted, which refuses to leave them alone. And they have to perpetuate against it a happiness that nobody shares. It is a freedom bound in chains.

This is because happiness is felt in relation to the Other (even when keeping the other at a distance): it is a shared state. Oblomov and Simeon still feel it, even though distanced from the collective, protecting, rather than sharing, their solitary contentment. We all do this by first seeking our own comfort, choosing to ignore the misery of others and shamelessly qualifying our indifference or impassibility. Average well-being (yours or mine – halfway between the ascetic's and the hedonist's) can only be born of a common culture, within a society's wealth and the interdictions that we perceive simultaneously as its radiance and its straitjacket. So it also comes with sacrifices that affect our most private selves: the irresistible attraction that I feel for a material or a colour, a cuisine or a sexual practice. How does this compare with the squabbles in which I must hedge my moral, political, artistic or literary convictions? Even if the majority of my peers are tolerant, including the Other in our well-being (and can we do otherwise?) is never without hardship. Whether I campaign with the organizers or the reformists, align myself with the tranquil individualists or slip into the passive majority or those who have chosen to cling to the values of the past, I must sacrifice part of myself to the practice, rule, law or opinion of this entourage or of my kin. This is the price we all pay for sociability and I pay, first and foremost, for my own *joie de vivre*.

There is no shortage of exhortations to sacrifice and submit in order to attain a certain kind of happiness. But available therapies also generate discomfort: throughout life we travel in a stretch of solitude that our activities never fully hide, and that are revealed to us by art. Doesn't each moment of conviviality toss us more cruelly into our solitude? Likewise music. Messiaen once suggested that music is 'an aesthetic of diversity' that also has the effect of changing our scenery. Music certainly conjures the enchantment of forgetting but, as the eponymous musician of Marguerite Yourcenar's novel *Alexis* says, 'We never know what it is going to tell us when it is finished.' Words are no better because 'they always break with something'. In his essay *Islands*, Jean Grenier invites us to partake in more knowledgeable practices, asking how we might fill the gap between man and the world: 'Ancient temples, churches, palaces, factories are the surest asylums from despair.' A delicate eudaemonism, composed of interrogations on happiness. One response is travel – not to escape but rather to locate ourselves – taken as a cure, like manual labour in monastic life or alcohol for painters.

In the end, the most salutary function of discomfort, whatever its guise, is to invite us on a quest for exaltation, to inspire action. The deceptive distance that separates the image of our well-being from our real contentment shows that life and well-being consist less in being happy than in wanting to be so. Bliss refers to a reality that remains by its nature absent and springs only from its own negation. But this irreducible distancing maintained by existence is also an *active* discomfort. It perpetuates itself according to the rhythm of our ardour to reduce it, which it also perpetuates. True danger lies in the passivity of which happiness willingly dreams. The words that commonly describe it – beatitude, serenity, satisfaction, quietude – are symbolic of a stabilized state, a sort of inertia where the body and soul are consumed by a lifelessness. The terms sluggishness and apathy could also apply. Well-being is an art, just like speaking or eating well, and it demands consistent attention if it is not to be destroyed. The expression 'moral comfort' is only shocking because of the lethargy it seems to invite. Oblomov, prostrate on his sofa, constantly imagines improving his tranquillity and eliminating whatever disturbs it, thus preventing his own satisfaction. Still, his pleasure is real and the nostalgic pursuit to which he is condemned unknowingly generates another comfort, concealed behind the one it aims to reduce.

The true pleasure of existence arises from the unflinching quest to achieve it. Far from preventing labour and pain, it fuels them and maintains the privation and subjection that we must choose according to taste – from asceticism to research or art, from manual labour to any other penchant or activity. Only they can provide us with this felicity. Rather than an already realized physical and moral state, it remains an image to overcome, not a here and now but a constantly repeated departure. If aspired to directly, this quest would provide nothing more than the sort of enraptured euphoria procured by tranquillizers. Its true nature lies in a fleeting representation and, even then, is only offered through perpetual provocation and reconstruction, and only out of the myriad trials I have referred to as discomfort.

The Austere School of Well-being

Throughout our lives, it is just such an alliance of joy and frustration that situates us in our homes. This is hardly surprising, as the reciprocal belonging that unites us with our homes leads to both. It is true that we are generally neither the architect nor the builder of our particular assemblage of stone and wood, cement and glass. Those who design and build it rely on the forms and know-how of their culture, faithful to a tradition. But as soon as the building becomes occupied, *lived in*, an anonymous dwelling is charged with a meaning it makes its own, linking all sorts of pleasant associations with the strong discomfort that I evoked earlier. Even if this inevitable element of displeasure – too much or too little sunlight, dampness, inadequate storage, an awkward staircase – makes our shelter costly, it still indicates how we can recognize ourselves and simultaneously feel ourselves its master and defenceless subject.

Even if we can see *how*, we do not know *why* there is this seemingly irreducible denial that everything (not only the home) is opposed to a well-being that is irreproachable. Is it one of those facts of civilization that sociologists and geographers use to explain our modes of existence? Indeed, the adjustment of a detail often causes a past betrayal to emerge, exposing its author to a rejection by the group and its practices. This can be the case even if there is an improvement because, regardless of whether a subjection is serious or inconsequential, it interferes in this vague but indivisible bliss we call well-being. Well-being refers to more than simple comfort. It includes the ensemble of a culture, and it integrates all its elements – pleasant or not – into an outline of daily happiness.

Well-being also acts as a ferrule: it seems probable that the least protective vernacular constructions (the Siberian hut, the nomad's tent, the Japanese house) toughen their occupants by teaching them to tolerate changes in weather instead of sparing them from them. This uncomfortable form of living well, which is varied and omnipresent, contributes to the universal (silent but uninterrupted) learning that houses and apartments implement. Integrated into our lifestyles, such learning perpetuates itself through the rigour of domestic rituals which, in some ways, sacralize it. It is maintained by the ongoing improvement of our homes, in that this constantly unattainable ideal of well-being remains asymptotic to our most costly realizations because of its true nature as an *inaccessible* image – it only exists beyond us.

The insufficiencies and servitude of domestic existence that we qualify negatively thus improve well-being by keeping our desire stimulated. True comfort, as I've said, does not reside in the negation of effort but in the reduction of its difficulty. The maladjustments that ethnologists and geographers blame at will on the home are those to which the ancients used to apply their wisdom – less in practices of defence against their milieu or kin than in welcoming and making use of dependencies they considered an inevitable accompaniment to their way of life, which they ritualized by usage. The bare Japanese interior seems beautiful to us even though it reiterates the ancient poverty of this people, now enriched with its essential values.

So, the action of dwelling always presupposes the diverse subjections where discomfort accompanies our pleasure. These include the representations involved in our quest for shelter, as well as the behaviours the shelter frames once it is occupied. Every approach to the acquisition of housing occurs image by image, from the first, still inchoate and uniquely pleasant, to the last, that accompanies every stage of the project. Our dream comes up against many barriers – finances, urban regulations, the diktats of our architect – and our place must emerge from all these encounters.

Daily gestures are another shared school of discomfort. The generational repetition of speech and gesture has turned bathing, bedtime, getting up, visits and meals into rituals. Whoever respects the sequence of these modest rituals partakes in them. They correctly 'play' the role that is expected of them on the perpetually anticipated 'stage' (of the bedroom, the bathroom, the living room, the dining room) and 'decor' (specified by its furnishings and utensils). They respect 'dialogues', displacements and gestures that are fixed by custom and therefore ineluctable.

These obligatory behaviours are ultimately pleasant. They primarily assure a perpetuation of existence. They also favour the practice of a generally agreeable conviviality and, in the framework of the household, a self-sufficient affectivity. Domestic ritual procures satisfaction from its own accomplishment, from faithfully following the rules. The gestures that characterize them were decided without our consultation and time may have erased their initial significance. They have become pure acts, accomplished for their own sake (the slightest omission would falsify the result), and to which we firmly attach our continuity as social beings.

As we are so dedicated to playing our part well, we accept the subjections or, rather, we see them as the inevitable flipside of greater joys. Whether I am starving or lacking appetite, I will come to the table at the appointed hour, and present to all the happy face that results from a good education. I will welcome a little-desired guest with a smile and undertake the rituals of hospitality, just as I would for my dearest friend. These constraints on my suffering stomach, my peace and quiet or my modest fortune will be sweetened due to a respect for the diverse satisfactions, pleasures and occasionally the true happiness of existence that they provoke. These practices oblige me, it is true, to accept certain sacrifices – a mediocre meal, uninteresting company, tasteless decor – but all it takes is for a loved one to arrive, for my presence to be necessary or simple courtesy to make me forego my liberty (to dress appropriately, to abstain from eating, to keep quiet, to stay at home or in another's company). I do this without a second thought and serenely accept it, as does everyone involved.

This seems to be one of the social functions of domestic rituals, of the individual subjection that any group of people bears. But being part of a group also brings about another form of serenity in that it provides security through a catharsis where personal tensions dissolve into conviviality. The rigorous sequence of these rituals of meal or visit diverts states of potential crisis by transforming the possible aggression of the participants into civility. The 'real', neutralized in a collection of symbols, ceases to terrorize the subject. By marking out our daily life and pacifying it at regular intervals, these rituals keep us in a present where gestures require constant attention, under the threat of exclusion from social life. Rituals maintain us in a reassuring symbolic order, and since we are concerned with accomplishing them correctly, we remain on the surface of our selves. Beyond their simple calming function, these rituals act like a drug, curbing our liberty to think of other things such as death. They do not preserve us from it, but from its image, and allow us to forestall the idea, every day, up until our last.

The temporary peace we obtain this way constrains our facility to choose. If we do not submit to these daily ceremonies in order to convert them into satisfactions (or at least into habits), their benefits escape us. Here again, the happiness of inhabiting only opens itself to us if we voluntarily and assiduously practise a certain discomfort, that can be more or less felt, but is assuredly inevitable.

eight
My Discomfort is My Culture

Such ambivalence of course extends beyond the home. All civilization everywhere displays a similar tendency, and with respect to everything. The negative side of this ambivalence (known as inconvenience, embarrassment, distress, fear or discomfort) consistently strikes us, whereas the positive side (known as comfort, well-being, agreement, euphoria or a certain kind of happiness) sometimes appears merely to be the inverse of the former, dependent on its retreat. A couple of true or misleading spoken words can be all that is necessary for this withdrawal; a new (and deceptive) assurance can spring from the occasionally formidable confusion they slip into ideas or acts. In an essay devoted to intellectual comfort, Marcel Aymé uses the term *revolution*, whose ambiguity has appealed just as strongly to those on the Left as to those on the Right. The Right rejoiced in 1940 when Marshal Pétain promoted a 'National Revolution' that allowed them to maintain their ideals and relieve their discomfort at being called 'reactionaries', since it meant they could also be considered 'revolutionaries'. Judges condemned Flaubert's *Madame Bovary* and Baudelaire's *Fleurs du mal* for the use of language that no longer shocks us. We have learned that poetry must generate a certain kind of distress or it will fail in its mission to feign the destruction of language, its signifying function and its consensual values. Ambivalence persists here and there, but a new use of words can cloak interior discomfort.

Perhaps something similar will happen in cyberspace, whose incomplete and illusory satisfactions I have already mentioned. Those who navigate the Internet abandon themselves to the vertigo of a sprawl lacking positions and distances, where everything is simultaneously close and far away, and where mobility extends to sitting in front of a computer. This is another, still poorly defined, way of thinking and travelling across a world, and one that serves the anonymous convenience of absolutely anybody. Who is to say that, were it structured differently, a new assurance could not surge from this uncertain space, where anything goes and everyone turns into a 'man without qualities' (which author Robert Musil understood as someone not frozen in their own character but open to all experiences)? But will we succeed in creating this new well-being without questioning time-honoured ways of thinking and acting, much like art and poetry do, by allowing the rich ambiguity of our essential values to shine through?

Comfort, discomfort and anti-comfort are the safest mooring for these values, which anchor every society across the earth and throughout history. In their own way, they lead to regret or to dreams, desires and projects based on the same principles (of the true, the beautiful, the efficient, the dream), defined by presence, change or absence. Well-being and ill-being are their signposts, which we see in the rituals that every private and public space imposes on its occupants and whose accomplishment simultaneously causes embarrassment and pleasure. But these 'places' only awaken these feelings through our private acceptance of the values that they embody, through our observation of the *code* that defines us, and only us, as the person for whom the message is destined.

Bruno Taut did not understand the codes of his Japanese house. Forgetting or rejecting them leads to a specific type of discomfort, yet opens the mind to a different kind of pleasure. The Scandinavian under his duvet or the Vietnamese on his bunk would see an exchange of their beds as an aberration. However, instead of just feeling physical discomfort they would take this as an affront to their national and everyday rituals. We only learn to judge comfort and discomfort as such, in relation to each other, and *together*, through culture.

But both comfort and discomfort are felt and delineated as images, and it is time to return to those levers that every civilization imposes on our thoughts and acts. Beyond the fact that images have become the ultimate merchandise, they smoothly guide our existence like a social catechism. More powerful than perception itself, they project people and things as a series of flashes instead of showing them in all their changeable reality, while their recurrence causes them repeatedly to act in the same way, which we can recall at will.

In my previous book *Habiter: rêve, image, projet* (Inhabiting: Dream, Image, Project) I showed the steady manner in which images condition our impressions of well-being, designing how we conceive, project, realize and improve it to our liking. But they have an equal effect on how we perceive discomfort, even when it does not simply reside in the imagination. Obviously, cold and heat, hunger and thirst, a poorly designed chair or uncomfortable interiors irritate our nerve endings before images take over. A physical malaise initially stems from messages sent from the senses to the brain, since it alone provides us with the consciousness (which we call sensation) of these initial emotional retorts. But our education, which has taught us to interpret our body according to our senses, takes over by awakening memories that are also presented as images.

When thinking of our future home, images guide our thoughts and they do so in a more imperious fashion the closer we get to its accomplishment: the project that will follow construction or purchase. Images reveal the possible states of discomfort in three ways: they function as *icons* of the uncomfortable object – through a relationship of simple resemblance they affirm its existence; they also suggest its *attributes* and *symbols* – a vulgar piece of furniture, the disgust that its possession would impose; a hard bed, the impending insomnia; a doubtful conviction, the aura of bitterness and approbation that will surround it. But beyond these assertions, images also determine the norms on which our judgements are based: their ever-similar return and their omnipresence remind us that what is anathema to us is not so for everybody. Images that emanate from a common culture carry some truth, and sometimes also legal obligations that it would be unreasonable to refuse. As such, they turn us into the accomplices of the precipitous staircase or the hard bed. They make the potentially avoidable discomfort seem tolerable, economical and practical and they turn something unsuitable, authorized by practices, norms and our means, into something inevitable and often desirable.

Thus lavishing appearance, components and rules on discomfort (and so stirring us to submission while justifying it), images accentuate it by eliminating our initial capacity to decide in the name of the codes by which we interpret them. When a magazine asserts that Louis XVI, the rustic, the romantic, the Japanese or Scandinavian style is the one that best suits me, the formidable authority of my entire culture weighs on my judgement and choice. The most venerable monuments, the most eminent professors or the least sophisticated weekly magazines that promote deliberate reversals of discomfort also limit the realm in which I can even conceive of it, as well as any personal effort on my part to reduce it. My pleasure will result less from a private need finally satisfied than from my subjection to norms predetermined by my education and culture. Discomfort is, first and foremost, heretical.

Because codes imbue images with an authority that submerges our judgement and taste, and that confirms their schematic character and steadiness, they command our decisions. Here again, the false well-being of conformity and consensus mask an inherent moral servitude. It is on their level that the recovery of discomfort operates. Each object of well-being has a meaning established by its uses, which becomes the orthodox way of perceiving it. Forgetting or negation only engenders the discomfort that has been defined for us, or at the very least an unorthodox use: a rug can cover furniture, decorate a wall, serve as a curtain or bedcover – only someone who knows the code walks on it and finds the sensation pleasing. Someone else might consider the chair I relax in to be an instrument of torture, or perhaps a mirror holder or a drying rack. Similarly, the curtain with which I conceal a corner of my room could be a tablecloth, rug or wall hanging.

Codes – of beauty and ugliness, misery and luxury, good and evil – are formed and subsist by and for social categories that maintain and control authority, via money and taste, rather than universal consent. In every society, this perversion of the real is expressed in the most profound and secret variety of discomfort, which is also the one we most tolerate, having been with us since our first day (along with the rest of our culture). At home, at school, in conversations and reading, we learned to see a *legitimate certainty* in it because it was founded on silence, custom and the law. Not the intimate and profound truth of the instinct and the body – which Nietzsche repeatedly called our 'great reason' – but still another, which all societies need for their self-definition, and to enable each individual to exist.

This also applies to me, in the world and in the home where these thoughts arose and where they now reach their conclusion. Doesn't this shelter act as the microcosm and metaphor for the human space that surrounds me, the network of ideas in which my thinking is activated from the sum of acts my energy is devoted to? Sitting beneath the roof of this home, I began to establish myself on the earth. Every room and every stage of my life dictates a distinct series of gestures, each one a way of being: labour, love, pleasure, travel, care for the body and soul. But the comfort and discomfort specified by my culture always accompany this common separation of my home and my existence; only the 'truth' of their codes defines my pleasures and privations.

Here I am still, on this cold, damp staircase that I did not design or build, but that initially stirred in me the idea of discomfort. My ancestors have charged the anonymity of the built thing with 'meaning' that makes it truly my own. Its handrail feels soft to my touch and its angles knowingly await my footsteps, but its inconvenience – which accompanies these joys and causes superficial hostility in me – has outlived generations, to the extent that it reveals the dual visage of my past. Its awkward but harmonious curve, still maintained by artisans from this province, reveals the thousands of compromises in which art and science endeavour to keep me; that is, my present. And I can no longer climb up or descend these stairs without recalling the (still unfulfilled) desire and the (never realized) project to make them more manageable, thus directing me towards the future.

So, the ordinary act of *inhabiting* the home with my body, and the world of the spirit beyond its walls, indicates that well-being and its absence are inseparable and timeless; they are irreducibly and ambivalently frozen in the 'form' of my civilization. But my taste for living and my quest for happiness stem from this familiar ambivalence. A faithful life companion, it exhibits only two sides – joy and pain, pleasure and subjection – and partakes in their common origin throughout society. My discomfort is my culture.

BIBLIOGRAPHY

Adorno, Theodor, and Walter Benjamin, *Correspondance 1928–1940, Adorno–Benjamin* (Paris, 2002)

Augé, Marc, *Non-lieux: introduction à une anthropologie de la surmodernité* (Paris, 1992)

The Confessions of St Augustine, trans. Rex Warner (New York, 1963)

Aymé, Marcel, *Le confort intellectuel* [1949] (Paris, 1967)

Bachelard, Gaston, *La poétique de l'espace* [1957] (Paris, 1974)

Bakhtin, Mikhail, *L'œuvre de François Rabelais* (Paris, 1970)

Balzac, *La comédie humaine* (1830–48)

Barragàn, Luis, *Discours de réception du prix Pritzker* (1980)

Bataille, Georges, *La part maudite* [1949] (Paris, 1990)

—, *La littérature et le mal* [1957] (Paris, 1994)

Baudelaire, Charles, 'L'invitation au voyage', in *Fleurs du mal* (Paris, 1857)

Benjamin, Walter, *Paris, capitale du XIXe siècle: le livre des passages* (Paris, 1989)

Bergson, Henri, *Matière et mémoire* [1897] (Paris, 1993)

Bloy, Léon, *Mon journal* [1896–1900] (Paris, 1963)

Boullée, Étienne Louis, *Architecture, Essai sur l'art* (Paris, 1968)

Céline, Louis Ferdinand, *Nord* (Paris, 1960)

Cervantes, Miguel, *Don Quixote*, trans. J. M. Cohen (Harmondsworth, 1950)

Chateaubriand, *Correspondance* [1815]

Conran, Terence, *Le grand livre de la maison* (Paris, 1985)

Crowley, John E., *The Invention of Comfort: Sensibilities and Design in Early Britain and Early America* (Baltimore, MD, 2001)

Defoe, Daniel, *Robinson Crusoe* (London, 1719)

Dumont, Louis, *Essais sur l'individualisme: une perspective anthropologique sur l'idéologie moderne* (Paris, 1983)

Fourier, Charles, *Le Phalanstère*, journal [1822]

Gallonio, Antonio, *Traité des instruments du martyre* [1591] (Grenoble, 2002)

Gandhi, Mohandas Karamchand, *The Story of My Experiments with Truth* [1927-9] (Boston, MA, 1993)

Gontcharov, Ivan, *Oblomov* [1858] (Lausanne, 1988)

Grenier, Jean, *Les îles* [1932] (Paris, 1977)

Haedens, Kléber, *Une histoire de la littérature française* [1954] (Paris, 1989)

Huguet, Edmond, *Dictionnaire de la langue française au XVIe siècle* (1925-67)

Kafka, Franz, 'A Hunger Artist' [1922], in *The Penal Colony: Stories and Short Pieces* (New York, 1958)

Kundera, Milan, *The Book of Laughter and Forgetting* (New York, 1980)

La Boétie, Etienne de, *Contr'un ou Discours de la servitude volontaire* (1574-1576)

La Fontaine, *Fables*, xi, 4: 'Le songe d'un habitant du Mogol' (1679)

La Rochefoucauld, *Réflexions ou sentences et maximes morales* (1664)

Laugier, Marc-Antoine, *Essai sur l'architecture* [1753] (Brussels, 1979)

Le Corbusier, *Manière de penser l'urbanisme* (Paris, 1946)

Ledoux, Claude Nicolas, *L'architecture considérée sous le rapport de l'art, des mœurs et de la législation* (Paris, 1804)

Maistre, Xavier de, *Voyage autour de ma chambre* (Lausanne, 1795)

Mallarmé, Stéphane, *Brise marine* (1866)

Matisse, Henri, *Écrits et propos sur l'art* (Paris, 1972)

Melville, Herman, *Moby-Dick; or, The Whale* (New York, 1851)

Messiaen, Olivier, in Jean Boivin, *La classe de Messiaen* (Paris, 1995)

Montaigne, *Essais*, I-21 and II-13, 20 (1595)

Musil, Robert, *L'homme sans qualités* [1930–33] (Paris, 1995)

Nietzsche, Friedrich, *On the Genealogy of Morality* [1887] (Oxford, 1996)

Nodier, Charles, *Examen critique des dictionnaires de langue française* (Paris, 1828)

Palladio, Andrea, *The Four Books of Architecture* [1570] (Cambridge, MA, 2002)

Pascal, *Pensées* (1670)

Pelletier, Philippe, *L'imposture écologique* (Montpellier, 1993)

Pezeu-Massabuau, Jacques, *Du confort au bien-être* (Paris, 2002)

—, *Habiter, rêve, image, projet* (Paris, 2003)
Rimbaud, Arthur, *Voyelles* (1871)
Rousseau, Jean-Jacques, *Émile* (1762)
Sade, *One Hundred Days of Sodom* (1778–87)
Tanizaki, Jun'ichiro, *Éloge de l'ombre* [1933] (Paris, 1977)
Taut, Bruno, *Houses and People of Japan* (Tokyo, 1937)
Verne, Jules, *Twenty Thousand Leagues Under the Sea* (1870)
—, *The Mysterious Isle* (1874)
Vitruvius, *Ten Books on Architecture* (Cambridge, 1999)
Weil, Simone, *L'attente de Dieu* (Paris, 1942)
Yourcenar, Marguerite, *Alexis, ou le traité du vain combat* [1929] (Paris, 1978)
Zola, Émile, *Les Rougon-Macquart* (1869–93)